His Holiness the

Dalai Lama

MIND *of* CLEAR LIGHT

Advice on Living Well and Dying Consciously

Translated and Edited by Jeffrey Hopkins, Ph.D.

ATRIA BOOKS

New York London Toronto Sydney

ATRIA BOOKS
1230 Avenue of the Americas
New York, NY 10020

Copyright © 2003 by His Holiness the Dalai Lama
and Jeffrey Hopkins, Ph.D.

Previously published as *Advice on Dying*

Library of Congress Cataloging-in-Publication Data

Bstan-'dzin-rgya-mtsho, Dalai Lama XIV, 1935–
[Advice on dying and living a better life]
Mind of clear light : advice on living well and dying consciously / His
Holiness the Dalai Lama ; translated and edited by Jeffrey Hopkins.
p. cm.
"Previously published as Advice on dying."
In English; translated from Tibetan.
ISBN 0-7434-6302-1 (hardcover)—
ISBN 0-7432-4469-9 (pbk. : alk. paper)
1. Death—Religious aspects—Buddhism. 2. Spiritual life—Buddhism.
I. Hopkins, Jeffrey. II. Title.

BQ4487.B77 2004
294.3'423—dc22
2004046410

First Atria Books trade paperback edition September 2004

10   9   8   7   6   5   4   3   2   1

ATRIA BOOKS is a trademark of Simon & Schuster, Inc.

Manufactured in the United States of America

For information regarding special discounts for bulk purchases,
please contact Simon & Schuster Special Sales at 1-800-456-6798
or business@simonandschuster.com.
ISBN: 978-0-7432-4469-5

Everyone dies, but no one is dead.

—TIBETAN SAYING

MIND *of* CLEAR LIGHT

Contents

Contents

Foreword

Tibet is known for profound insights into the depths of the mind. A repository for Buddhist teachings, Tibet has long maintained traditions of practice and instruction centered on manifesting these deep states of mind and making use of them for spiritual progress. I began my own instruction in these systems at a Tibetan and Mongolian monastery in New Jersey at the end of 1962. While living at the monastery for nearly five years, I learned the Tibetan language, meditated, and studied a broad range of topics. This allowed me, upon return to the monastery in the summer of 1968, to appreciate the magnificent expositions of subjects—large and small—

by an aged lama, Kensur Ngawang Lekden, who had been the abbot of a Tantra monastery in Lhasa, the capital of Tibet, when the Communist Chinese invaded in 1959. In the course of his teachings, the lama spoke several times of a profound book about death that he had with him. He explained that the book was most helpful in approaching death because it described in detail the deepening mental states through which the dying person passes and how to prepare for them. He added that we pass through these states each and every day when we go to sleep or end a dream, as well as during fainting, sneezing, or orgasm.

I was fascinated.

From the lama's brief references to the contents of this book, I could see that our usual level of consciousness was superficial compared to these deeper states. Wanting to learn more, I asked him to teach me the text, but he put it off. Eventually, in 1971, I left on a Fulbright fellowship to study for a few months with one of the lama's Tibetan students, who was teaching in Germany at the University of Hamburg. There I stayed in what was actually a large closet. A friend of the Tibetan scholar had built a narrow bed above the window in the closet, with a small ladder up to it and a tiny desk under it. One night fairly early in my stay, the lama appeared to me in a thrilling dream in the shining form of his six-year-old self without the pockmarks he had on his adult face. Standing on my chest, he announced, "I will be back." I knew then he had died.

I proceeded to India, where I stayed for over a year, attending two series of teachings by His Holiness the Dalai Lama, having long discussions with him in many audiences, receiving private teachings, translating a text he had written on the topic of dependent-arising and emptiness, and interpreting for a group of students who had asked for an audience. Upon returning to the United States, I went directly to the monastery in New Jersey, intent on going through Lama Kensur Ngawang Lekden's effects to find the book about dying.

To my delight, I found it!

I read the book and requested teaching on it from two lamas. It has had a profound influence on me. It describes both the superficial and profound levels of mind so vividly that it allows one to imagine going deeper and deeper within the mind, on the ultimate journey of transformation. Knowing that this material would be valuable for many people, I asked His Holiness the Dalai Lama if he would provide commentary on another text on the same topic, a poem written by the First Panchen Lama in the seventeenth century (which also has a commentary by the author of the book on dying I had read). I suggested to the Dalai Lama that in this way a more accessible book could be made, and he agreed.

A few days later, I was called to His Holiness's inner office and sat across from him with a tape recorder. Drawing from a wide range of traditions and experiences to explain the text, His Holiness discussed in vivid detail the structure of Buddhist depth psychology as well as the process of dying and the period after death and before the next life. He described how competent yogis manifest the profound levels of mind for spiritual transformation. He spoke movingly about the value of being mindful of death, the ways to do so, how to overcome fear while dying and also in the intermediate state between lives, and how to help others who are dying. His teachings are the heart of this book.

To give you an idea of the impact the Dalai Lama had on me that day, let me quote some notes from my book, *Cultivating Compassion,* where I am discussing meditating on the nature of reality:

The Dalai Lama advises that you do this type of meditation on someone or something that you value highly, so the experience of emptiness will not be misinterpreted as a devaluing of the subject—the value will remain high but will be seen in a different way. During a period when he was teaching me in his office in India, my experience was particularly intense. One late afternoon as I looked at him across his desk with a set of windows stretching behind him, the sun was fairly low on the horizon in Kangra Valley. Our topic was the stages of death—a profound presentation of deeper stages of the mind, on which not just death but all conscious experience is built. In Tibetan the Dalai Lama has incredible powers of speech—very fast and very clear at the same time—and brings a vast array of teachings to bear on a single topic. The scene was brilliant with the glow of the sun across a vivid orange sky—like the second stage of the four subtle minds experienced when dying. I felt as at-home as I ever could in my life. As I stepped out of his office, I was awe-struck by the snow-covered peak above Dharmsala: I began walking down to my room farther down the mountain, passing a place with a view of a mountain on the other side, too; the space between the two mountains was filled with a rainbow that formed a complete circle. It was amazing! Several days later, I was leaving after my last class with the Dalai Lama, preparing to return to the States. As I stepped near the door he said, "It is like a dream." I said, "What?" "It's like a dream," he replied. Even in this most vivid and valuable period of my life, he caused me to reflect on the emptiness of this valuable experience. Emptiness does not cancel phenomena; on the contrary, it is quite compatible with effectiveness, and with value.

IMPACT OF THE TEACHINGS

The Dalai Lama's teaching is replete with detail about the actual process of dying, and also with practical advice. I gained many insights into the gradual collapse of consciousness and learned much that later turned out to be very useful.

While my father and mother were vacationing at

their small winter home in Florida, my father had a stroke; he was eighty-one. I was far away in Vancouver, teaching at the University of British Columbia, so when my three brothers went to Florida to visit my ill father, I stayed in Vancouver. We were all very relieved when my father rose from his comatose state and even returned home. However, by the time I arrived a few weeks later, after my brothers had left, my father was back in the hospital, comatose again.

One day he was lying on his back and he opened his eyes. He turned and we began gently talking. At one point with a playful gleam in his eyes, he said, "You wouldn't believe what's going on in this hospital." Wondering what he meant, I happened to look up at the television at the foot of his bed. A steamy hospital soap opera was on, and I noticed that the hospital had put a small speaker on his pillow. While in his coma he had heard all those shows! After a while, I told him the source of his ideas, and later turned off his speaker, remembering the Dalai Lama's teaching that near the time of death it is most valuable to have someone remind you of virtuous thoughts.

A few days later, my father took a turn for the worse and slipped into a deep coma. Visiting one night, I found that the hospital had moved him to a different room. This time the television was blasting out a quiz show. I wanted to turn it off, but was told by the nurse that it was a favorite of the nearly deaf man in the other bed. Confounded, I sat at the foot of my father's bed wondering what to do. The TV roared a question about a ship that had sunk at sea, so I figured that at least I could engage the other man. "Do you know the name of that ship?" I shouted. When he did not move a muscle, I realized that he was comatose, too. But my father sat up in bed and said, "The *Andrea Doria*." He was lucid, and had been listening all along!

I turned off the TV, and we went on to have a nice conversation. He was his usual contented self. He asked for crackers and milk, which the nurse provided in a particularly tender way. We chatted for a while, and as I left, I said, "Shall I say hello to Mother?" "You bet," he replied cheerfully.

The hospital called my mother early the next morning to tell her that my father had died during the night. How relieved I was that before he died, he had come to his senses with his spirits restored. And that the TV was silent.

The hospital had left my father's body in his room,

alone. I went there and, remembering not to disturb the body, sat and kept silent because I did not know his particular vocabulary of religious belief. Just by being there I felt I could support him on his journey.

A year later, my mother suffered what was probably a stroke. She dialed the home of my brother Jack and his wife, Judy. Jack was away, and when Judy answered, Mother said she felt terrible, had a headache, and kept talking in a scattered way. She said she felt faint and might be sick. Then her voice faded away. Since Mother did not hang up, Judy ran to the house next door and called the rescue squad. Subsequently, the hospital brought her back from death's door three times, each time leaving her struggling to communicate. Seeing her incoherent struggle, I remembered that the Dalai Lama had spoken of the need for friendly advice that could evoke a virtuous attitude, and approached her bedside. I knew that her special word was "spirit," so I said, "Mother, this is Jeff. Now is the time for the spirit." She immediately settled down and stopped struggling. I gently repeated, "Now is the time for the spirit." A few days later, she died peacefully.

When my cousin Bobby was diagnosed with brain cancer, he spoke at length about his illness with my brother Jack, who asked him if there was anything he would like to do while he was still active. Bobby said, "I'd like the cousins to gather and tell stories about Grandpa." My paternal grandfather was a powerful man who protected his family, farm, church, and all of his involvements in vigorous and even humorous ways. So Jack gathered us together, all fourteen of us. We all knew Bobby was dying and did not pretend otherwise, but we certainly were not morose about it either. Most of us had hilarious stories to tell, which I videotaped.

Bobby's sister, Nancy, called me and asked for advice on what to do near the time of death. "Make sure no one is weeping and moaning around him," I told her. "Make things simple. Turn off the TV. Let people come say good-bye before the end has begun."

On Bobby's next-to-last day, the family watched the video of the cousins' gathering and put it away. The next day, with everything kept simple and quiet, he died.

The Dalai Lama advises that as we near the end we need to be reminded of our practice, whatever kind it is. We cannot force on others our views, or a higher level of practice than what they can manage. When my friend Raymond knew he was dying of AIDS, he and his partner asked me what they should do. Remembering my parents' deaths and my own paralysis and near death from Lyme disease, I knew that long after we become unable to interact with others, we can have a strong, lucid interior life. During my extreme illness I internally repeated a mantra that I had recited over the course of almost thirty years. I found that despite not being able to communicate with others, I could repeat the mantra with unusual lucidity. Occasionally I would try to speak, but failed. Despite failing, I did not worry. That would have been a big mistake. I just kept repeating the mantra, which put me at ease.

Bearing in mind my own experience, I suggested to Raymond that he choose a saying that he could repeat over and over again. He chose a four-line stanza by Joseph Goldstein:

May I be filled with loving-kindness.
May I be well.
May I be peaceful and at ease.
May I be happy.

I thought his choice might be too long, but I knew it was right for Raymond, since it was what he wanted.

Raymond practiced his mantra. His partner put it

into a plastic frame by his bedside, so when Raymond turned his head, he saw it and was reminded to repeat it. Later, when Raymond returned from the hospital to die, he gradually became withdrawn, losing the power of speech, then losing the ability to point with his hand, and finally losing the capacity to move at all. Yet when I went into his room, sat on the floor by his bed, and gently said, "May I be filled with loving-kindness," his face would light up and his eyes moved under his closed eyelids. It had worked!

THE FIRST PANCHEN LAMA

In this book, His Holiness the Dalai Lama draws on a vast array of Indian and Tibetan textual and oral traditions to explain a seventeen-stanza poem by the First Panchen Lama. The Dalai Lama unpacks the meaning of the stanzas, one by one, by giving a detailed presentation of the stages of death, the intermediate state between lives, and the rebirth, all the while describing their practical application in a very moving way.

The poem that is at the heart of this study was written in the seventeenth century. Its importance and revelance have been transmitted by monastics and laypersons in Tibet and now throughout the world. But to take for granted the ability to study and to practice it is to be blind to the current state of religion in Tibet, the situation of the Panchen Lama, and the ongoing tension between Tibet and China.

Therefore, I would like to discuss the history of the titles Dalai Lama and Panchen Lama and the line of incarnations of the author of the poem, the First Panchen Lama. I also want to clear up several misunderstandings about the situation in Tibet and discuss the current incarnation of the Panchen Lama, who is under house arrest in China.

In the mid-thirteenth and early-fourteenth century, Tsongkhapa Losang Drakpa founded a spiritual tradition in Tibet called Geluk, also known as the Yellow Hat School. Around 1445, a student of Tsongkhapa, Gendun Drup, built a large monastery, called Tashi Lhunpo (Mount Luck), in Shigatse, in a province west of Lhasa, the capital of Tibet. Gendun Drup retroactively came to be called the First Dalai Lama when the third incarnation in his line, Sonam Gyatso (1543–1588), received the name "Dalai" (a Mongolian translation of "Gyatso," meaning "ocean") from his Mongolian patron and follower, Altan Khan, in 1578.

Gendun Drup also received the name "Panchen" from an erudite Tibetan contemporary, Bodong Choklay Namgyel, when he answered all of the latter's questions. "Panchen" means "great scholar," from the Sanskrit word "pandita," meaning "scholar," and the Tibetan word "chen po," meaning "great." Successive abbots of Tashi Lhunpo Monastery, who were elected and served limited terms, were all called "Panchen."

In the seventeenth century, the Fifth Dalai Lama gave Tashi Lhunpo Monastery to his teacher, Losang Chokyi Gyeltsen (1567–1662), the fifteenth abbot of the monastery. As abbot of the monastery, he was called "Panchen." However, when Losang Chokyi Gyeltsen died, the Fifth Dalai Lama announced that his teacher would reappear as a recognizable child-successor, so his line of incarnations retained the title "Panchen Lama" and became the abbots of Tashi Lhunpo Monastery. The title "Panchen Lama" switched from being an elected one for a specific term to a line of reincarnations.

Since that time it has been a convention in Tibet for the Dalai Lama and Panchen Lama to be involved in the recognition of each other's successor to varying degrees. The Dalai Lama is the general spiritual and temporal leader of Tibet, whereas the Panchen Lama is the leader of that particular area around Shigatse. The history of how the Dalai Lama and the Panchen Lama received their names undercuts the ludicrous claims made by the current government of China that somehow their titles indicate subservience to Chinese authority. The titles are completely homegrown. To further support its claims of legitimacy, Beijing points to the fact that the Panchen Lama is called "Erdini." However, this is a Mongol word meaning "precious jewel," and is a complimentary title shared with many Mongolian lamas. In the case of the Panchen Lama, it was conferred on him in 1731 by the Emperor Kiang-shi, a Manchurian who at that time controlled China.

We need to keep in mind that at different times in its history China was ruled by Mongolian and Manchurian outsiders, as well as by Han Chinese. In the early twentieth century Dr. Sun Yat-sen, the founding father of modern China, promoted the fabrication of a unified Middle Kingdom including Manchuria, Mongolia, East Turkestan, Tibet, and China. However, in 1911 even he said that when the nationalist revolution defeated the Manchu dynasty, China had been occupied twice by *foreign* powers—first by the Mongolians and later by the Manchurians. The Mongolians, Manchurians, and the

Han Chinese all considered Tibet to be a foreign land even when, as a powerful neighbor, their empires occasionally interfered in Tibet. We need also to be aware that in the eighth century the Tibetan Empire reached even to the capital of China, Ch'ang-an, known today as Xian. So, if occasional incursions into a country mean that the aggressor owns that country, then it could be argued that Tibet owns China.

Beijing seeks to legitimize its rule in Tibet by establishing that it plays a crucial role in the identification of the region's important lamas, the most prominent being the Dalai Lama and the Panchen Lama. Beijing's desperate attempts to pretend relevance in Tibet's religious affairs are mirrored in the series of events surrounding the recent identification of the Eleventh Panchen Lama. In the interest of clarification, let me briefly explain the process of searching for a high reincarnation.

1. Inquiries are made throughout the country about special signs occurring upon the birth of children, about mothers who had unusual dreams, and about children who have special knowledge without being taught.
2. Portents are analyzed. For instance, after the death of the previous Dalai Lama a rainbow pointed east,

suggesting rebirth in the eastern part of the country. Then, two objects like tusks about a foot high appeared on the eastern side of the deceased Dalai Lama's reliquary. After a search party had found the next incarnation, flowers bloomed in winter at an outdoor amphitheater where the Dalai Lama lectures, and people in Lhasa spontaneously began singing a tune that contained the names of his parents. (Many portents pass without being noticed at the time and are understood only later.)

3. Supernormal sources of knowledge are consulted. A party is sent to a lake southeast of Lhasa that evokes prophetic visions. In the case of the present Dalai Lama, the party saw in the lake a picture of the monastery near his birthplace as well as a picture of his own house. They also saw three letters, "A, Ka, Ma," that indicated the province ("A" for the Amdo Province), the monastery ("Ka" for Kumbum Monastery), and the Dalai Lama's own name ("Ma," which stood for "female," since the Dalai Lama as a child had a female name, Long Life Goddess).

4. A divination is performed by rotating a bowl with dough-balls containing the names of the final candidates until one spins out.

5. Search parties are sent out in disguise to test candidates for special knowledge and to see whether they
can identify articles belonging to the previous lama.
In the case of the present Dalai Lama, he identified
one of the disguised members as a monk-official and
another as a monk from Sera Monastery. The articles he had to choose from were two rosaries, two
small ritual drums, and two walking sticks.

The idea of a materialistic Communist government
becoming involved in such a religious process is laugh-
able, but this is exactly what happened as the following
events concerning the identification of the present
Panchen Lama indicate.

CHRONOLOGY OF THE IDENTIFICATION
OF THE ELEVENTH PANCHEN LAMA

1984: The Chinese Communist government, which
invaded eastern Tibet in 1950 and completed its
occupation of all sections in 1959, announces that
it will allow Tibetans to search for incarnations of
high lamas.

1987: The Chinese government establishes a special school in Beijing for reincarnate lamas to produce "patriotic lamas, who would cherish the unity of the motherland."

January 28, 1989: The Tenth Panchen Lama dies at age fifty-one at Tashi Lhunpo Monastery in Shigatse, Tibet, four days after delivering a message criticizing the Chinese government in which he says, "Chinese rule in Tibet has cost more than it has benefited." He had stayed behind in Tibet after the March 1959 escape by the Dalai Lama, and had been imprisoned and tortured for nine years and eight months during the Cultural Revolution after making a report sharply critical of Chinese policy in Tibet. (After his death there were recurrent and persistent rumors that he had been poisoned.) The same day the Dalai Lama proposes sending a ten-person religious delegation to Tibet to make prayers at the Panchen Lama's monastery.

February 1989: Li Peng, Prime Minister of China, announces that outsiders—meaning Tibetans in exile—would not be allowed to "meddle in the selection procedure."

August 1989: The Chinese government announces a five-point plan for the search, selection, and recognition of the Panchen Lama. The plan is a compromise with authorities at the Panchen Lama's monastery and includes the Chinese government's insistence that a lottery be included in the process and that they arrange the final public confirmation. A search committee is appointed by Beijing, led by Chadrel Rinpochay, abbot of the Panchen Lama's monastery, who is known to be cooperative with the Chinese.

March 21, 1991: The Dalai Lama informs the Chinese government through its New Delhi embassy that he wishes to assist in the search for the Panchen Lama's reincarnation by sending a delegation to the lake of prophetic visions, southeast of Lhasa.

June 1991: Three months later the Chinese government responds that there is no need for interference.

July 17, 1993: The head of the search party as constituted by the Chinese government, Chadrel Rinpochay, sends offerings and a letter to the Dalai Lama concerning the Panchen Lama reincarnation. He explains that a party has visited two lakes and received confirmation that the Panchen Lama has reincarnated.

August 5, 1993: The Dalai Lama sends a reply to Chadrel Rinpochay through the Chinese embassy in

Delhi inviting the delegation to visit him in India to discuss the search for a reincarnation. There is no response.

October 17 and 18, 1994: The Dalai Lama, in a private meeting with a Chinese individual who has close ties to the Chinese government, says he is waiting for a reply to his letter to Chadrel Rinpochay of August 5, 1993. He stresses the importance of searching for the reincarnation according to traditional religious procedures.

January 1995: The same Chinese individual is reminded twice about the above discussion.

April 1995: The Chinese government announces that it has implemented new legislation concerning the search, selection, and approval of incarnations of high lamas.

May 14, 1995. After performing extensive analysis of over thirty children, receiving four prophecies from oracles, and performing nine divinations including the dough-ball ritual, the Dalai Lama formally recognizes a six-year-old boy, Gedhun Choekyi Nyima, born on April 25, 1989, in the Lhari District of Nagchu, Tibet, as the Eleventh Panchen Lama. The timing accords with an auspicious date in the calendar of the Wheel of Time teachings, which have a special connection with the Panchen Lama. The Dalai Lama and Chadrel Rinpochay's delegation (appointed by Beijing) are in agreement.

May 15, 1995: A Chinese official news agency attacks the Dalai Lama's statement.

May 17, 1995: The Beijing government holds Chadrel Rinpochay incommunicado along with his fifty-year-old secretary, Jampa, in Chengdu for twelve days. The boy lama is taken into custody by the Chinese authorities. At the age of six he is the world's youngest political prisoner.

May 19, 1995: Wall posters begin to appear in Tibetan towns denouncing the Chinese government's interference in the selection of the Panchen Lama.

May 21, 1995: Chinese authorities in Tibet call meetings in Lhasa, Shigatse, and Nagchu to announce a ban on gatherings of more than three people and to prohibit public discussion of the Panchen Lama's reincarnation. Party cadres move into Tashi Lhunpo Monastery to run reeducation sessions, at which time monks are invited to criticize Chadrel Rinpochay. The boy lama and his family, as well as two other children who were leading candidates, disappear and are reported to have been moved to Beijing. In Lhasa, all leading figures in the government and the religious hierarchy are required to participate in meetings denouncing the Dalai Lama's statement.

May 24, 1995: An emergency three-day session of the Chinese People's Political Consultative Conference issues a statement describing the Dalai Lama's statement as "illegal and invalid."

May 1995: Tibet's leading dissident and former political prisoner, Yulu Dawa Tsering, is instructed to report to the police every other day.

June 11, 1995: Chadrel Rinpochay's business manager, Gyara Tsering Samdrup, is detained by Chinese authorities in Dingri on suspicion that he communicated with the Dalai Lama.

July 12–13, 1995: Foreign tourists are expelled from Shigatse, the seat of the Panchen Lama's monastery, so that they cannot observe demonstrations. Tibetans are prevented from performing religious activities at the Panchen Lama's monastery, including even devotional circumambulation of temples and religious sites.

To date, the whereabouts of the boy recognized by the search party from his own monastery and by the Dalai Lama as the Panchen Lama, is unknown. As of

2002, he and his parents have been held for seven years by the Chinese government, which refuses international observers access to the boy to assess his well-being. The head of the search party, Chadrel Rinpochay, was released from seven years' incarceration in prison in 2002.

In what can only be called a surreal turn of events, the central Communist Chinese government appointed its own search party and declared it had found the real Panchen Lama. The president of China, Jiang Zemin, took a keen interest in the process. The governmentally approved substitute, now thirteen years old, has been featured prominently in Chinese newspapers as a patri-otic scholar capable of inspiring devotion. In 2001, the Beijing-supported pseudo–Panchen Lama announced on a tour of the prosperous eastern seaboard, "I deeply understand the greatness of the Communist Party of China now and feel the warmth of the socialist family under the glorious policy of the Chinese Communist Party."

SUGGESTIONS

Why is the Beijing Communist government so worked up over this issue? It is trying to bring legitimacy to its invasion of Tibet by showing the world that it plays a vital role in the spiritual life of the nation. It may also have been trying to announce the discovery of the new Panchen Lama at the thirtieth anniversary of China's naming what is actually part of Tibet the "Tibetan Autonomous Region." However, the Dalai Lama and the delegation from the Panchen Lama's monastery that was originally appointed by Beijing came to agreement on the same candidate, and the Dalai Lama announced the identification, no doubt to preempt Chinese interference.

Beijing also makes the totally unfounded claim that the previous Chinese government, the Guomintang, was involved in the identification of the present Dalai Lama. However, this flies in the face of ample historical evidence. When the enthronement of the Dalai Lama took place on February 22, 1940, the Chinese emissary, Wu Zhongxin, was treated like the other envoys from Bhutan, Sikkim, Nepal, and British India, and had no special role to play. The Guomintang made absurd claims that the boy bowed to Beijing and that the Chinese emissary set the boy on the throne. Even a Tibetan official who was present at the enthronement and who has cooperated with the Chinese government, Ngabo Nawang Jigme, Vice Chairman of the Standing Committee of the People's Congress, said on July 31, 1989, "We, the Communist Party, need not tell lies based upon Guomintang lies." At that time, Comrade Chang Feng of the United Front Ministry said, "In future, we will not say that Wu Zhongxin officiated at the enthronement of the Fourteenth Dalai Lama." Today, in desperation, Beijing has reverted to the Guomintang fabrication. Tellingly, despite the fact that Tibet has large monastic universities delving into all manner of philosophical issues, there has never been a word in the Tibetan language for a country that includes both Tibet and China.

The policy of the present Chinese government toward Tibet is based on disregard and neglect of the needs and wishes of the Tibetan people. This must be reversed by indicating to Beijing in clear terms that the world does indeed take this issue seriously. Governments and nongovernmental organizations should urge the Chinese authorities to free the Panchen Lama and those connected with his discovery, to allow him to be educated at his own monastery, and to allow him to travel freely. The United Nations should back the Dalai Lama's efforts to negotiate a settlement about the status of Tibet.

Tibetan culture extends far beyond Tibet, stretching from Kalmuck Mongolian areas near the Volga River (in Europe where the Volga empties into the Caspian Sea), Outer and Inner Mongolia, the Buriat Republic of Siberia, Bhutan, Sikkim, Ladakh, and parts of Nepal. In all of these areas, Buddhist ritual and scholastic studies are conducted in Tibetan. Youths came from throughout these vast regions to study in Tibet, especially in and around its capital, Lhasa, usually returning to their native lands after completing their studies (until Communist takeovers in many of these countries). Thus, Tibetan culture is central to a vast area of Inner Asia, and its demise has far-reaching implications.

This book should remind us of the treasures of Tibet.

Jeffrey Hopkins, Ph.D.
Professor of Tibetan Studies
University of Virginia

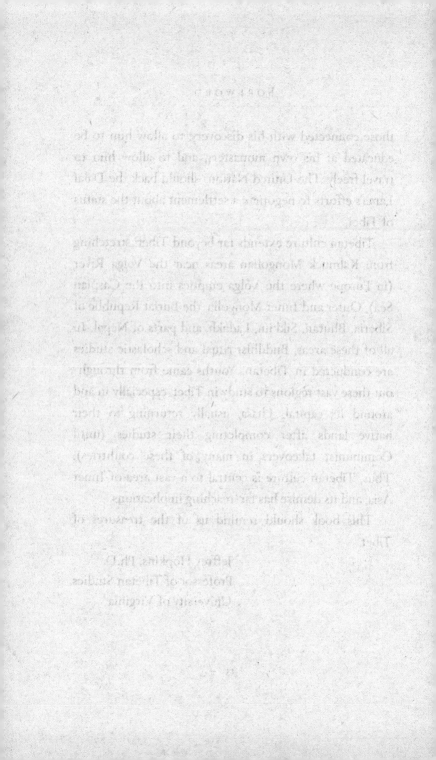

MIND *of* CLEAR LIGHT

I

Awareness of Death

Just as when weaving
One reaches the end
With fine threads woven throughout,
So is the life of humans.

—BUDDHA

It is crucial to be mindful of death—to contemplate that you will not remain long in this life. If you are not aware of death, you will fail to take advantage of this special human life that you have already attained. It *is* meaningful since, based on it, important effects can be accomplished.

Analysis of death is not for the sake of becoming fearful but to appreciate this precious lifetime during which you can perform many important practices. Rather than being frightened, you need to reflect that when death comes, you will lose this good opportunity for practice. In this way contemplation of death will bring more energy to your practice.

You need to accept that death comes in the normal course of life. As Buddha said:

A place to stay untouched by death
Does not exist.
It does not exist in space, it does not exist in
    the ocean,
Nor if you stay in the middle of a mountain.

If you accept that death is part of life, then when it actually does come, you may face it more easily.

When people know deep inside that death will come but deliberately avoid thinking about it, that does not fit the situation and is counterproductive. The same is true when old age is not accepted as part of life but taken to be unwanted and deliberately avoided in thought. This leads to being mentally unprepared; then when old age inevitably occurs, it is very difficult.

Many people are physically old but pretend they are young. Sometimes when I meet with longtime friends, such as certain senators in countries like the United States, I greet them with, "My old friend," meaning that we have known one another for a long period, not necessarily physically old. But when I say this, some of them emphatically correct me, "We are not old! We are long-time friends." Actually, they *are* old—with hairy ears, a sign of old age—but they are uncomfortable with being old. That is foolish.

I usually think of the maximum duration of a human life as one hundred years, which, compared to the life of the planet, is very short. This brief existence should be used in such a way that it does not create pain for others. It should be committed not to destructive work but to more constructive activities—at least to not harming others, or creating trouble for them. In this way our brief span as a tourist on this planet will be meaningful. If a tourist visits a certain place for a short period and creates more trouble, that is silly. But if as a tourist you make others happy during this short period, that is wise; when you yourself move on to your next place, you feel happy. If you create problems, even though you yourself do not encounter any difficulty during your stay, you will wonder what the use of your visit was.

Of life's one hundred years, the early portion is spent as a child and the final portion is spent in old age, often just like an animal feeding and sleeping. In between, there might be sixty or seventy years to be used meaningfully. As Buddha said:

> Half of the life is taken up with sleep. Ten years are spent in childhood. Twenty years are lost in old age. Out of the remaining twenty years, sorrow, complaining, pain, and agitation eliminate much time, and hundreds of physical illnesses destroy much more.

To make life meaningful, acceptance of old age and death as parts of our life is crucial. Feeling that death is almost impossible just creates more greediness and more trouble—sometimes even deliberate harm to others. When we take a good look at how supposedly great personages—emperors, monarchs, and so forth—built huge dwelling places and walls, we see that deep inside their minds was an idea that they would stay in this life forever. This self-deception results in more pain and more trouble for many people.

Even for those who do not believe in future lifetimes, contemplation of reality is productive, helpful, scientific. Because persons, minds, and all other caused phenomena change moment by moment, this opens up the possibility for positive development. If situations did not change, they would forever retain the nature of suffering. Once you know things are always changing, even if you are passing through a very difficult period, you can find comfort in knowing that the situation will not remain that way forever. So, there is no need for frustration.

Good fortune also is not permanent; consequently, there is no use for too much attachment when things are going well. An outlook of permanence ruins us: Even if you accept that there are future lives, the present becomes your preoccupation, and the future takes on little import. This ruins a good opportunity when your life is endowed with the leisure and facilities to engage in productive practices. An outlook of impermanence helps.

Being aware of impermanence calls for discipline— taming the mind—but this does not mean punishment, or control from the outside. Discipline does not mean prohibition; rather, it means that when there is a con- tradiction between long-term and short-term interests, you sacrifice the short-term for the sake of long-term benefit. This is *self*-discipline, which stems from ascer- taining the cause and effect of karma. For example, for the sake of my stomach's returning to normal after my recent illness, I am avoiding sour foods and cold drink that otherwise appear to be tasty and attractive. This type of discipline means protection. In a similar way, reflection on death calls for self-discipline and self-protection, not punishment.

Human beings have all the potential to create good things, but its full utilization requires freedom, liberty. Totalitarianism stifles this growth. In a complementary way, individualism means that you do not expect something from the outside or that you are waiting for orders; rather, you yourself create the initiative. Therefore, Buddha frequently called for "individual liberation," meaning self-liberation, not through an organization. Each individual must create her or his own positive future. Freedom and individualism require self-discipline. If these are exploited for the sake of afflictive emotions, there are negative consequences. Freedom and self-discipline must work together.

BROADENING YOUR PERSPECTIVE

From a Buddhist perspective, the highest of all aims is to achieve Buddhahood in order to be capable of helping a vast number of sentient beings; however, a medium level of achievement can liberate you from the painful round of birth, aging, sickness, and death; a lower, but still valuable level of achievement is the improvement of your future lives. From the gradual improvement of your lives liberation can be attained, and based on this, eventually Buddhahood can be attained. First, your perspective extends to include future lives; then by thoroughly understanding your own plight, your perspective deepens to include all of the round of suffering from one life to another, called cyclic existence or samsara. Finally this understanding can be extended to others, through the compassionate wish that all sentient beings be freed from suffering and the causes of suffering. This compassion drives you to aspire to Buddhahood.

You have to be concerned with deeper aspects of life that affect future lives before understanding the full nature of suffering and cyclic existence. This understanding of suffering, in turn, is required for the full development of compassion. Similarly, we Tibetans are seeking to achieve a measure of self-rule in Tibet in order to be of service to the beings in our homeland, but we are also striving to establish ourselves in a refugee situation in India. The accomplishment of the former, greater purpose depends upon our accomplishing the latter, temporary aim.

DISADVANTAGES OF NOT BEING MINDFUL OF DEATH

It is beneficial to be aware that you will die. Why? If you are not aware of death, you will not be mindful of your practice, but will just spend your life meaninglessly, not examining what sorts of attitudes and actions perpetuate suffering and which ones bring about happiness.

If you are not mindful that you might die soon, you will fall under the sway of a false sense of permanence "I'll die later on, later on." Then, when the time comes, even if you try to accomplish something worthwhile, you will not have the energy. Many Tibetans enter a monastery at a young age and study texts about spiritual practice, but when the time comes to really practice, the capacity to do so is somehow lacking. This is because they do not have a true understanding of impermanence.

If, having thought about how to practice, you make a decision that you absolutely have to do so in retreat for several months or even for many years, you have been motivated by your knowledge of impermanence. But if that urgency is not maintained by contemplating the ravages of impermanence again and again, your practice will peter out. This is why some people stay in retreat for years but experience no imprint on their lives afterward. Contemplating impermanence not only motivates your practice, but also fuels it.

If you have a strong sense of the certainty of death and of the uncertainty of its arrival, you will be motivated from within. It will be as if a friend is cautioning, "Be careful, be earnest, another day is passing."

You might even leave home for the monastic life. If you did, you would be given a new name and new clothing. You would also have fewer busy activities; you would have to change your attitude, directing your attention to deeper purposes. If, however, you continued busying yourself with the superficial affairs of the moment—delicious food, good clothing, better shelter, pleasant conversation, many friends and acquaintances, and even making an enemy if someone does something you do not like and then quarreling and fighting—you would be no better off than you were before you entered the monastery, and perhaps even worse.

Remember, it is not sufficient to withdraw from these superficial activities out of embarrassment or fear of what your friends who are also on the path might think; the change must come from within. This is true for monks and nuns as well as lay people who take up practice.

Perhaps you are beset by a sense of permanence, by thinking that you will not die soon and that while you are still alive, you need especially good food, clothing, and conversation. Out of desire for the wondrous effects of the present, even if they are of little meaning in the long run, you are ready to employ all sorts of shameless exaggerations and devices to get what you want—making loans at high interest, looking down on your friends, starting court proceedings—all for the sake of more than adequate provisions.

Since you have given your life over to such activities, money becomes more attractive than study, and even if you attempt practice, you do not pay much attention to it. If a page falls out of a book, you might hesitate to retrieve it, but if some money falls to the ground, there is no question. If you encounter those who have really devoted their lives to deeper pursuits, you might think well of that devotion, but that would be all; whereas if you see someone dressed in finery, displaying his or her wealth, you would wish for it, lust after it, hope for it—with more and more attachment. Ultimately, you will do anything to get it.

Once you are intent on the fineries of this life, your afflictive emotions increase, which in turn necessarily bring about more bad deeds. These counter-productive emotions only lead to trouble, making yourself and those around you uncomfortable. Even if you briefly learn how to practice the stages of the path to enlightenment, you acquire more and more material things and get involved with more and more people to the point where you are, so to speak, practicing the superficialities of this life, meditatively cultivating desire for friends and hatred for enemies and trying to figure out ways to fulfill these afflictive emotions. At that point, even if you hear about real, beneficial practice, you are apt to feel, "Yes, that is so, but . . ." One "but" after another. Indeed, you have become accustomed to afflictive emotions throughout your beginningless cyclic existence, but now you have added on the very practice of superficiality. This makes the situation even worse, turning you away from what will really help.

Driven by such lust, you will find no comfort. You

are not making others happy—and certainly not yourself. As you become more self-centered—"*my* this, *my* that," "*my* body, *my* wealth"—anyone who interferes immediately becomes an object of anger. Although you make much out of "*my* friends" and "*my* relatives," they cannot help you at birth or at death; you come here alone, and you have to leave alone. If on the day of your death a friend could accompany you, attachment would be worthwhile, but it cannot be so. When you are reborn in a totally unfamiliar situation, if your friend from the last lifetime could be of some help, that too would be something to consider, but it is not to be had. Yet, in between birth and death, for several decades it is "*my* friend," "*my* sister," "*my* brother." This misplaced emphasis does not help at all, except to create more bewilderment, lust, and hatred.

When friends are overemphasized, enemies also come to be overemphasized. When you are born, you do not know anyone and no one knows you. Even though all of us equally want happiness and do not want suffering, you like the faces of some people and think, "These are *my* friends," and dislike the faces of others and think, "These are *my* enemies." You affix identities and nicknames to them and end up practicing the generation of desire for the former and the generation of hatred for the latter. What value is there in this? None. The problem is that so much energy is being expended on concern for a level no deeper than the superficial affairs of this life. The profound loses out to the trivial.

If you have not practiced and on your dying day you are surrounded by sobbing friends and others involved in your affairs, instead of having someone who reminds you of virtuous practice, this will only bring trouble, and you will have brought it on yourself. Where does the fault lie? In not being mindful of impermanence.

ADVANTAGES OF BEING MINDFUL OF IMPERMANENCE

However, if you do not wait until the end for the knowledge that you will die to sink in, and you realistically assess your situation now, you will not be overwhelmed by superficial, temporary purposes. You will not neglect what matters in the long run. It is better to decide from the very beginning that you will die and investigate what is worthwhile. If you keep in mind how quickly this life disappears, you will value your time and do what is valuable. With a strong sense of the imminence of death, you will feel the need to engage in spiritual practice, improving your mind, and will not waste your time in various distractions ranging from eating and drinking to endless talk about war, romance, and gossip.

All beings want happiness and do not want suffering. We use many levels of techniques for removing unwanted suffering in its superficial and deep forms, but it is mostly humans who engage in techniques in the earlier part of their lives to avoid suffering later on. Both those who do and do not practice religion seek over the course of their lives to lessen some sufferings and to remove others, sometimes even taking on pain as a means to overcome greater suffering and gain a measure of happiness.

Everyone tries to remove superficial pain, but there is another class of techniques concerned with removing suffering on a deeper level—aiming at a minimum to diminish suffering in future lives and, beyond that, even to remove all forms of suffering for oneself as well as for all beings. Spiritual practice is of this deeper type.

These techniques involve an adjustment of attitude; thus, spiritual practice basically means to adjust your thought well. In Sanskrit it is called *dharma,* which means "that which holds." This means that by adjusting counter-productive attitudes, you are freed from a level of suffering and thus *held back* from that particular suffering. Spiritual practice protects, or holds back, yourself and others from misery.

From first understanding your own situation in cyclic existence and seeking to hold yourself back from suffering, you extend your realization to other beings and develop compassion, which means to dedicate yourself to holding others back from suffering. It makes practical sense for you, just one being, to opt for taking care of many, but also, by concentrating on the welfare of others, you yourself will be happier. Compassion diminishes fright about your own pain and increases inner strength. It gives you a sense of empowerment, of being able to accomplish your tasks. It lends encouragement.

Let me give you a small example. Recently, when I was in Bodh Gaya, I fell ill from a chronic intestinal infection. On the way to the hospital, the pain in my abdomen was severe, and I was sweating a great deal. The car was passing through the area of Vulture Peak (Buddha taught here) where the villagers are extremely poor. In general, Bihar State is poor, but that particular area is even more so. I did not even see children going to or coming from school. Just poverty. And sickness. I have a very clear memory of a small boy with polio, who had rusty metal braces on his legs and metal crutches up to his armpits. It was obvious that he had no one to look after him. I was very moved. A little later on, there was an old man at a tea stop, wearing only a dirty piece of cloth, fallen to the ground, left to lie there with no one to take care of him.

Later, at the hospital, my thoughts kept circling on what I had seen, reflecting on how sad it was that here I had people to take care of me but those poor people had no one. That is where my thoughts went, rather than to my own suffering. Though sweat was pouring out of my body, my concern was elsewhere.

In this way, though my body underwent a lot of pain (a hole had opened in my intestinal wall) that prevented sleep, my mind did not suffer any fear or discomfort. It would only have made the situation worse if I had concentrated on my own problems. This is an example from my small experience of how an attitude of compassion helps even oneself, suppressing some degree of physical pain and keeping away mental distress, despite the fact that others might not be directly helped.

Compassion strengthens your outlook, and with that courage you are more relaxed. When your perspective includes the suffering of limitless beings, your own suffering looks comparatively small.

2

Liberation from Fear

Your life dwells among the causes of death
Like a lamp standing in a strong breeze.

—NAGARJUNA'S *PRECIOUS GARLAND*

The First Panchen Lama wrote a seventeen-stanza poem that many Tibetans use to focus their daily reflections on dying. The title of the poem is: *Wishes for Release from the Perilous Straits of the Intermediate State, Hero Releasing from Fright*. In order to be freed from frightful straits, such as being beset by robbers, thugs, or wild animals, you need a heroic and capable guide to save you. Similarly, to be liberated from the terror of illusory appearances while dying and during the intermediate state between lives, you need to practice the advice offered in this poem, which provides profound techniques for release from those fears. By reflecting on the poem you learn how death occurs, knowledge that will be useful during the actual process. Dying is a time when the deeper levels of mind manifest themselves; daily reflection also opens the door to those states.

The poem contains a series of wishes to be used by any of us so that when death strikes, the mind will react in a virtuous way. Some seek to generate a powerful virtuous motivation at the time of death to fortify and activate virtuous predispositions, which leads them to a favorable rebirth. Their goal is the attainment of a good transmigration into the next lifetime to continue their religious practice. Others, as we will see, seek to utilize the deeper levels of mind manifested during dying to achieve more advanced spiritual states. All practitioners aim to be of service to others.

The First Panchen Lama's poem describes three levels of spiritual practice—for the most highly trained, the middling, and the least—in the form of wishing to be aware during the process of death, the state between lives, and rebirth. He speaks in detail about what you should do at each stage. You need to adopt an appropriate level of practice for the remainder of your life so that at the time of dying you will move successfully through each stage.

When death actually comes, if you are not used to this practice, it will be very difficult to succeed at any beneficial reflection. Therefore, now is the time to practice and prepare, while you are still happy and the circumstances of your life are in accord. Then, at the time of real need and pressure, there will be no worry. If, when you have time to hear, think, meditate, and ask questions, you do not make preparation, on the last day there will be no time and you will be without protector or refuge, with nothing left but regret. It is better long before that time to institute a continuous practice of reflection on the process of death and the intermediate state between lives—imagining the steps so they become familiar. This is very important, for then you can achieve success in keeping with your greatest capacity.

Mere knowledge of the process of death and practices concerned with it is not sufficient; you must gain familiarity with these over months and years. If now, when the senses are still clear and mindfulness has not degenerated, your mind is not made serviceable to and familiar with the way of virtue, it will be difficult—when dying—for the mind to proceed of its own accord on a strange path. When dying, you may be physically weak from illness and mentally depressed from terrible fear.

Therefore, it is necessary to become intimate with the practices related to dying. There is no substitute. There is no pill.

The effort it takes to apprehend these practices depends upon internal motivation arising from the conviction that experiences of pleasure and pain directly correspond to your own virtuous and nonvirtuous actions. Thus, in the beginning it is important to develop an understanding of the cause and effect of actions, or karma, founded on the knowledge that good actions stem from a tamed mind, and bad actions stem from an untamed mind. Though virtuous and nonvirtuous actions are performed by body, speech, and mind, the mind is the most important, so the root of Buddhist practice is transformation of the mind. The emphasis of Buddhist teaching is on a tamed mind—the foundation of which is the perception that you are the creator of your own pleasure and pain. As Buddha said:

> Buddhas do not wash away ill deeds with water,
> Nor remove transmigrators' sufferings with their
>   hands,
> Nor transfer their realizations to others.

Beings are freed through the teachings of the
truth, the nature of things.

You are your own protector; comfort and discomfort
are in your own hands.

The Status of the Lineage of the Panchen Lamas

The First Panchen Lama, whose name was Losang Chokyi
Gyeltsen, was a tutor of the Fifth Dalai Lama in the seventeenth century. Prior to that time, even though he was
an ordinary monk, the local people and his own teacher
considered him to be an incarnation of a great Tibetan
yogi, Ensaba. He may not have been one of the greatest
scholars, but he was a great practitioner. Like his teacher
Sangyay Yeshay, he had genuine respect for the other line-
ages of Buddhist practice. In the Collected Works of his
teacher, we can see religious vocabulary from other traditions, and this openness must have influenced Panchen
Losang Chokyi Gyeltsen's own practice. He certainly
made a great contribution to the mutual respect of and
harmony between Tibetan schools of Buddhism.

The previous Panchen Lama, Lobsang Trinley Lhundrup Choekyi Gyeltsen, the tenth in the line of reincarnations, died in 1989. He and I were both born in the northeastern province of Tibet called Amdo. At the time of choosing him as the reincarnation of his predecessor there was a little controversy. The officials of his monastery in Shigatse, which is in western Tibet, were in the Amdo Province in an area under a Muslim warlord's sphere of influence. They decided that he was the true reincarnation of the Ninth Panchen Lama. In the Seventeen Point Agreement that the Chinese government promoted as a way to establish a relationship with Tibet, the Chinese indicated, or perhaps insisted, that the Tibetan government must recognize this boy, who was already in their hands, as the Tenth Panchen Lama. In this way, his recognition was a little controversial, but he himself proved that he was a great hero, courageous in the service of Tibetan Buddhism and the Tibetan people. There is no doubt.

When I first met him around 1952, he was very innocent, very sincere, and very bright. In 1954, the year when we both went to China, he came from western Tibet to join me in Lhasa, the capital, for a few days. He proceeded on to China through the Amdo Province, and I went through Kongpo. Perhaps due to the disgruntlement of some of his officials, his attitude changed a little.

In 1956, at the celebration of Buddha's 2500th birthday when we were both in India, there were still small indications of this. However, because very sad events—battles with Chinese troops—took place in 1957 and 1958 in the two eastern provinces, Amdo and Kham, information about atrocities carried out by the Chinese army finally reached him. He then fully realized, perhaps belatedly, that all Tibet must unite and face this new threat. At my final scholastic examination, he sent a trusted monk-official, who explained to me that at present the Panchen Lama's thinking had changed a great deal because of recent news from the area of his own birthplace. Under this new threat, he was completely determined that his monastery at Shigatse work together with the Tibetan government.

After my escape from Tibet to India in 1959, the Panchen Lama took my place as the leader within Tibet and for the next several years acted wonderfully. Eventually he was put under house arrest and imprisoned. After he was freed, he wisely used the opportunity, expending every effort to improve the situation for the Buddhist religion and Tibetan culture. By "wisely" I mean that he did not touch sensitive issues such as the independence of Tibet, but instead simply put all of his energy into preserving Buddhism and Tibetan culture. Sometimes he even publicly scolded Tibetans who wore only Chinese-style clothing and spoke only Chinese. Those Tibetans were pressured into wearing Tibetan dress and speaking Tibetan. Through such actions he proved himself.

His death was very sudden and untimely. I was greatly saddened. While he was alive, there was one Tibetan as a leader speaking inside the country on behalf of the people, while I served from the outside as much as I could. After losing him, now there is no one inside who can do what he did. They are either too old or too frightened. His death was a great loss.

As soon as he passed away, I sent a message to the Chinese government saying that I wanted to dispatch a spiritual delegation to make some offerings at the Panchen Lama's monastery, but they declined to allow it. After a couple of years I asked the Chinese government to allow a spiritual delegation to search for the Panchen Lama's reincarnation, but again they declined.

Obviously, the important point was that the Panchen

Lama's reincarnation should be authentic. At that time, some Tibetans urged that the reincarnation had to be found outside occupied Tibet, but I considered their motive to be political. What really mattered was to find the genuine reincarnation, whether inside or outside Tibet. If the reincarnation were inside Tibet, I knew it would be necessary to discuss this with the Chinese government, so I wanted to send a spiritual delegation to search for the reincarnation.

That request was rejected, but in the meantime, through an informal, private channel, I developed contact with a lama, Chadrel Rinpochay, who sent a list of over twenty-five candidates along with several pictures. As soon as I saw the picture of Gedhun Choekyi Nyima, I had a feeling of affinity, of intimacy. I did some divinations, which were very positive for him. Finally, I performed a divination circling a bowl with dough-balls containing the names of the final candidates on strips of paper rolled up inside them. It was as if his flew up out of the bowl. Through these steps, I made the decision that he is the reincarnation of the Tenth Panchen Lama.

However, I did not make an announcement. As time passed, more and more Tibetans, especially from inside Tibet, urged me to make the decision. I kept trying to communicate with the Chinese government but without result. Finally, I thought that it would be appropriate to make the announcement on the date when Buddha first gave teachings on Kalachakra, or Wheel of Time, with which the Panchen Lama has a special connection. I made another divination through the use of dough-balls as to whether I should make the announcement or not, and it was positive.

I made the announcement, and the next day I received a big scolding from our masters, the Chinese government. But what was indeed frightful was that within a few days the young reincarnation, together with his parents, was taken from his birthplace to Lhasa, and from there to China, and since then, there has been no news of them. I feel very sad about this, because the effects of what were, from the Chinese government's viewpoint, my illegal activities had to be suffered by the child.

The Chinese believe that they should be the final authority. Such did indeed happen a few times in Tibetan history when there was internal disagreement between groups in the Tibetan community about a narrowed down choice of candidates. They turned to the Chinese emperor, who was both a Buddhist and a patron of Tibetan Buddhism, to make the final decision in front of an image of Shakyamuni Buddha through using a golden vessel, out of which a name written on a stick was drawn. Those were cases of Tibetans' doing away with ecclesiastical argument in a religious way.

My predecessor, the Thirteenth Dalai Lama, was chosen unanimously by the Tibetan government after the usual internal procedures without any outside consultation. When he, in turn, was asked about the Ninth Panchen Lama, he declared his choice among the candidates, but he was too young to be completely authoritative. Since Tibetans gravitate to whatever the easier way is, they turned to the outside consultation of the golden vessel, which was performed by the Chinese ambassador. Still, the name to which the Thirteenth Dalai Lama had given his strong recommendation came forth from the golden vessel.

Because Tibetans trusted the Chinese emperor, it is natural that they would involve their patron and supporter in certain important religious activities. That type of situation has completely changed nowadays with the current Chinese government, whose primary interest is control. Regarding the present Panchen Lama, they performed a golden vessel divination to make their own choice of another new Panchen Lama, but it was predetermined—they already had him and his parents waiting in the temple for the public announcement. Then the Chinese government put the monk—who, acting as the leader of Tibetan Buddhism, "chose" the stick—under house arrest. This is certainly totalitarianism.

Nevertheless, on two or three occasions I have seen videos of the Chinese government's official Panchen Lama, Gyaltsen Norbu, and he seems okay. In one video he was performing a teaching in connection with a long-life ritual. He knew the ceremony by heart and explained the meaning of the long-life ritual very well.

OVERVIEW OF THE POEM

The First Panchen Lama's seventeen-stanza poem is a guide to specific Buddhist techniques for overcoming fear of death and for potentially utilizing the stages of dying for spiritual advancement. It is my hope that this description of the inner, psychological experiences and physical changes will provide helpful reflection for those concerned about death and the deeper levels of the mind, and that it will serve as a source of information for scientists interested in working with Buddhist scholars and yogis on issues around dying. Whereas scientists usually have viewed mind as a product of the body, certain specialists are beginning to think of the mind as a more independent entity that can affect the body. It is obvious that strong emotions, such as hatred, can affect the body, but now experiments are being conducted in connection with specific practices of intentionally training the mind, such as the development of faith, compassion, single-pointed concentration, reflection on emptiness, or special meditations in the Nyingma tradition of Tibetan Buddhism. These experiments show that mental training can have an autonomous function, influencing the body, even desensitizing it. I think that consultation with nurses, especially at hospices, about impending signs of death also would be fruitful.

The first seven stanzas of the Panchen Lama's poem explain how to approach dying. After an initial stanza about taking refuge in Buddha, his Doctrine, and the Spiritual Community (explained in this chapter) the next two stanzas (Chapter Three) address the importance of valuing the present lifetime as an opportunity for spiritual practice. They describe how to make use of this precious situation by reflecting on the impermanence of the present in order to undermine our excessive attachment to fleeting experiences. Stanzas four and five (Chapter Four) speak to adopting a perspective that can handle both the overwhelming suffering that can accompany the time near death and the delusions that appear while dying. Stanzas six and seven (Chapter Five) prescribe how to achieve the most favorable conditions for death by remembering what to practice and by remaining joyful.

The next three stanzas (Chapter Six) describe at length the appearances that occur during the first four phases of dying and how to meditate throughout them. This section calls on our knowledge of the collapse of the physical elements that support consciousness and their corresponding experiences. These gradually open the way for three deeper, subtle minds to manifest themselves as described in the following stanza (Chapter Seven). This chapter lays out the structure of mind and body according to Highest Yoga Tantra. Stanzas twelve and thirteen (Chapter Eight) address the culminating experience of the fundamental innate mind of clear light. This innermost level of mind is the basis of all conscious life.

The last four stanzas (Chapters Nine and Ten) describe the intermediate state (after death and before the next life) and show how to react to the often horrific events that can occur during that state. They detail how various levels of practitioners can seek to direct their ensuing rebirth.

Together these seventeen stanzas present the full scope of preparation for death by removing unfavorable conditions, gaining favorable conditions, learning how to engage in spiritual practice while dying, learning how to handle the intermediate state between lives, and influencing the subsequent rebirth.

The Beginning of the Poem:
Obeisance to Manjushri

Before the poem begins, the First Panchen Lama first makes an expression of worship, an obeisance, to Manjushri, the physical manifestation of the wisdom of all Buddhas. The author considers Manjushri to be undifferentiable from his own lama, or teacher. The reason why he offers obeisance to Manjushri is as follows.

The root of a good death and a good intermediate

state between lives, and even the attainment of Buddhahood over a continuum of lifetimes, is successful practice of the clear light of death. There are two classes of practice: compassion and wisdom. The practice of the clear light during death is included within the practice of wisdom; therefore it is contained within the stages of teaching of the profound view of the compatibility of appearance with the emptiness of inherent existence—the transmission of which stems from our kind teacher Shakyamuni Buddha through Manjushri. (The stages of teachings on vast compassionate motivations and deeds were similarly transmitted from Shakyamuni Buddha, but through Maitreya and Avalokiteshvara.) Thus, since the successful practice of death and the intermediate state between lives is mainly concerned with the factor of wisdom, the First Panchen Lama makes an expression of worship to Manjushri:

Obeisance to the Guru Manjushri.

Having paid obeisance to the manifestation of wisdom, he begins the poem itself.

Stanza One

I and all beings throughout space and without exception
Go for refuge until the ultimate of enlightenments
To the past, present, and future Buddhas, the Doctrine,
    and the Spiritual Community.
May we be released from the frights of this life, the
    intermediate state, and the next.

Within an attitude of self-help, Buddhists go for refuge to the Buddha as the teacher, to Buddha's Doctrine (states of realization and teachings of them) as actual refuge, and to the Spiritual Community as guides to that refuge. They develop conviction that internalizing the doctrine can offer protection from suffering. They consider these Three Jewels (Buddha, his Doctrine, and the Spiritual Community) to be the final refuge.

Seeking refuge only to relieve your own suffering and attain liberation from cyclic existence does not fulfill the qualifications of altruistic refuge. Your perspective would not be vast. Your attitude of refuge should be for the sake of all sentient beings, for their freedom from suffering and attainment of Buddhahood. You should seek the omniscience of Buddhahood in order to fulfill the primary aim—to help others.

You should consider all sentient beings throughout space and seek to attain the ultimate, or supreme, of enlightenments, which surpasses that of more narrowly focused practitioners because it involves the removal of obstructions not just to liberation from cyclic existence but also to omniscience. This ultimate of enlightenments, or supreme nirvana, is beyond the extremes of bias either in the direction of being caught in the cyclic existence of the repeated round of birth, aging, sickness, and death (called samsara) or of inactive peace, a state of liberation from the round of suffering without full capability of helping others.

The First Panchen Lama advises that his readers go for refuge to the Buddha, his Doctrine, and the Spiritual Community in order to attain the highest enlightenment for the sake of other sentient beings. This is called causal refuge; you are taking refuge in the Three Jewels that are established in the mental continuums of others—placing your confidence especially in the cessations of suffering and the spiritual states they have actualized to overcome their suffering. Petitioning those who possess the Three Jewels evokes their compassion—not by generating it in them but by opening yourself to it.

By taking causal refuge you are practicing the doctrines taught by the Teacher Buddha with the Spiritual Community of high realization as your model; you are actualizing spiritual paths and many levels of the cessation of suffering. In this way, you yourself become a member of the Spiritual Community of high realization, gradually removing all obstructions to liberation from cyclic existence, and obstructions to omniscience—becoming a Buddha. You are released from all frights and have attained omniscience, so that you know other people's dispositions and understand which techniques will help them. For the sake of attaining such a *resultant* refuge, this stanza petitions the three *causal* sources of refuge to invoke their compassion.

Since refuge is the beginning of Buddhist practice, the first wish in the Panchen Lama's text is concerned with it. Without refuge, it is difficult for other practices to be successful. However, an attitude of complete confidence in the Three Jewels is not sufficient in itself. As Buddha said, "I teach you the path to liberation. Know that liberation itself depends on you." Buddha is just the teacher of the path. He does not give realization like a gift; you have to practice morality, concentrated meditation, and wisdom.

Consider, for example, recitation of the mantra *om mani padme hum* (pronounced "om mani padmay hum"), which is practiced for the sake of invoking compassion within yourself for all types of sentient beings. After finishing a session of repetition—twenty-one, a hundred and eight, or more times—the value of the practice is dedicated through reciting a prayer in connection with Avalokiteshvara, since he is the physical manifestation of the compassion of all Buddhas:

Through the virtue of this practice,
May I quickly attain a state
Equal to that of Avalokiteshvara
In order to help all sentient beings attain
    the same.

There is no possibility of attaining Buddhahood merely through reciting *om mani padme hum,* but if your practice is conjoined with real altruism, it can serve as a *cause* of attaining Buddhahood. Similarly, if you touch, see, or listen to a qualified guru, it can have positive impact, which can be helpful in developing deeper spiritual experience. When my senior tutor, Ling Rinpochay, and I would touch foreheads at the beginning of a more formal meeting or at other times when I would take his hand and touch it to my forehead, emotionally this would give me a strong, intimate feeling related to greater faith and trust. In Buddha's time, when someone who really respected and loved him touched his feet, this certainly would bring some benefit. But if someone who had no faith or respect in Buddha even grabbed his leg and pressed his or her head against it, there probably would not be any blessing. Though something is required from the guru's side, mainly it is from the side of the disciple.

There was a truly wonderful lama from the Amdo Province of Tibet who, when asked for a blessing by putting his hand on the practitioner's head, would say, "I am not a lama who can bestow liberation by placing a hand—that has the nature of suffering—on top of someone's head."

SUMMARY ADVICE

1. The motivation for your practice should be the benefit of all living beings—their freedom from suffering and attainment of perfection. Always adjust

your motivation toward helping others as much as possible. At least try to do no harm.

2. Buddhas are teachers of the spiritual path; they do not give realization like a gift. You have to practice morality, concentrated meditation, and wisdom on a daily basis.

3

Preparing to Die

Not knowing that I must leave everything and depart,
I did various ill deeds for the sake of friend and foe.
—BUDDHA

Stanza Two

*May we extract the meaningful essence of this life
   support*
*Without being distracted by the senseless affairs of this
   life,*
*Since this good foundation, hard to gain and easy to
   disintegrate,*
*Presents an opportunity of choice between profit and
   loss, comfort and misery.*

You need both internal and external favorable conditions for the consummation of successful practice, and
you already have these. For instance, as humans we have

a body and mind that supports our understanding of teachings. Thus, we have met the most important internal condition. Externally, you need transmission of the practices and the freedom to practice. If, possessing these circumstances you exert yourself, you are guaranteed success. However, if you do not exert yourself, it is a tremendous waste. You must value these conditions, for when they are not present, you do not even have an opportunity. You should value your current endowment.

Since you have attained a human body as well as the right external circumstances, then, with an aspiration to practice, you can make your life worthwhile. You must do so. It is time to do so. If with this opportunity you work on beneficial causes, you can achieve many powerful ones; if, motivated by the three poisons of lust, hatred, and bewilderment, you work on nonvirtuous causes, you can similarly achieve very powerful bad actions in many forms.

It is very difficult for other beings, such as animals, who do not have our excellent human foundation, to achieve virtues through their own power. There are rare cases of their doing something virtuous given the right external conditions, but it is hard for them to think. When animals act out of lust or hatred, they do so temporarily or superficially; they are incapable of bad physical and verbal actions in great strength and in many varieties. However, humans can think from a great many points of view. Because our intelligence is more effective, humans can achieve good and bad on a grand scale.

If this human endowment is used for good, it can be very powerful. If you take care and work at good actions, the aims of this life and those of future lives can be achieved. If you do not take care, your bad actions can induce tremendous suffering. This is why, although many types of beings have evolved on this planet since its formation, those who have brought about the most improvement are human beings, and those who have learned how to create the most fear, suffering, and other problems—threatening even the destruction of the planet—are also humans. The best is being done by humans, and the worst is being done by humans. Since you have the physical endowment required for achieving profit and loss, comfort and misery, you must know how to use it unerringly.

If you knew you would have this endowment of choice throughout a long continuum of lives, perhaps it would be all right not to use it wisely in this life. However, this is not the case. Changeability in any phenomenon is a sign that it depends on causes, so the commonly experienced changeability of our body is a sign that it, too, depends on causes. Elements from your father and mother are involved as causes and conditions of your body, but for your mother's ovum and father's sperm to come together, still other causes are required. For instance, these depend on the ovum and sperm of their parents and so on, back to the ovum and sperm of some sentient beings after the formation of this world. Still, if the establishment of this body of flesh and blood depended only on ovum and sperm, then, since ovum and sperm were not present at the time of the formation of this world-system and since they did not arise causelessly (given the consequence that then they would have to appear either everywhere at all times or never), this means that there are also other factors—this being karma.

Each world-system has eras of formation, continuation, disintegration, and finally a period of voidness. After this fourfold sequence, a new world-system forms from the circulation of winds, or energies, and from subsequent development of other elements. Whether this process is explained in accordance with current scientific views or Buddhist philosophy, there is a time when a specific world-system does not exist. The process of the formation of a world-system begins in dependence upon many causes and conditions, which themselves are caused phenomena. These phenomena must be made either by a creator deity or by the force of the karma (former actions) of the persons who will be born there and will experience and use that environment. From a Buddhist viewpoint it is impossible for what is caused, and thus impermanent (including a world-system), to depend for its creation on the supervision, or motivating force, of an uncaused and thus permanent deity. Rather, it is by the force of sentient beings' karma that the process of formation of the environment takes place. The only other choice is that it is uncaused, which would be absurd.

Just as the environment is produced and disintegrates in dependence on causes and conditions, the same is true for the quality of life of sentient beings. It is a firm rule of cause and effect that, in the long term, good causes produce good results and bad causes produce bad results. This means that any long-term good effect is preceded by the accumulation of a good cause. Similarly, to produce a powerful effect, it is necessary to have a powerful cause. With regard to our human physical nature, or life support, it was necessary for us in our former lives to have accumulated the manifold powerful causes and conditions that individually produced the shape, color, clarity of senses, and other qualities of this body.

If after having performed a virtuous action and accumulated its potency, that potency remained without degenerating until its fruit issued forth in either this or a future life, it would not be so fragile. But that is not the case. Rather, the generation of a strong nonvirtuous state of mind, such as anger, overpowers the capacity of a virtuously established potency so that it cannot issue forth, much like scorching a seed. Conversely, the generation of a strong virtuous attitude overpowers potencies established by nonvirtues, making them unable to issue *their* effects. Thus it is necessary not only to achieve many powerful constructive causes but also to avoid contrary forces that would cause those beneficial causes to degenerate.

The good actions required for accumulating these causes, or potencies, arise from a tamed mind, whereas bad actions arise from an untamed mind. Common beings like us have been accustomed to an untamed mind since beginningless time. Given this predisposition, we can conclude that actions performed with an untamed mind are more powerful for us and actions performed with a tamed mind are weaker. It is important to appreciate that this excellent life support of a human body that we now possess is a wholesome result of many powerful good actions from a tamed mind in the past. It was very difficult to gain, and since it is very rare you must take care to use it well, making sure that it is not wasted. If it was not rare, not difficult to gain, you would not have to take care, but this is not the case.

If this human endowment, so difficult to attain, were stable and permanent—not prone to deterioration—there would be time later to make use of it. However, this life-support system is fragile and easily disintegrates from many external and internal causes. Aryadeva's *Four Hundred Stanzas on the Yogic Deeds of Bodhisattvas* says that once the body depends on the four elements of earth, water, fire, and wind, which themselves oppose each other, physical happiness is just an occasional balance of these elements, not an enduring harmony. For instance, if you are cold, heat is at first pleasant, but then too much heat has to be avoided. The same is true of diseases; medicine for one ailment can eventually bring on another malady, which then has to be counteracted. Our bodies are sources of great trouble and complications; physical happiness is merely the temporary absence of such problems.

Our bodies must be sustained by gross sustenance, food, but when you eat too much, the very thing needed to create health becomes a source of sickness and pain. In countries where food is scarce, hunger and starvation are great causes of suffering, but in those countries where it is plentiful in many nutritious varieties, there is still suffering from overeating and indigestion. When there is balance without any manifest problems, we call this "happiness," but it would be foolish to think that we had become, or could ever become, free from disease. This kind of body is a home for problems. It is not as if in the absence of disease, or wars, or starvation, we would not die. The nature of the body is to disintegrate. Right from conception, the body is subject to dying.

So this human body is a precious endowment, potent and yet fragile. Simply by virtue of being alive, you are at a very important juncture, and carry a great responsibility. Powerful good can be achieved for yourself and others, so becoming distracted by the minor affairs of this lifetime would be a tremendous waste. You should make wishes to use this lifetime in this body effectively and make petitions to your guru, the three refuges, and other sources of help in doing so, thereby urging yourself on from the inside and seeking assistance from the outside. To this end, do not just recite the words of this stanza, but reflect on their meaning, causing it to appear to your mind.

In sum, since this human body, which supports your life, is beneficial, was difficult to gain, and is easy to disintegrate, you should use it for your benefit and that of others. Benefits come from a tamed mind: When your mind is peaceful, relaxed, and happy, external pleasures such as good food, clothing, and conversation make things even better, but their absence does not overpower you. If your mind is not peaceful and tamed, no matter how marvelous the external circumstances are, you will be burdened by frights, hopes, and fears. With a tamed mind, you will enjoy wealth or poverty, health or sickness; you can even die happily. With a tamed mind, having many friends is wonderful, but if you have no friends, it is all right, too. The root of your own happiness and welfare rests with a peaceful and tamed mind.

In terms of others, when you have a peaceful and tamed mind, life is more pleasant for your friends, spouse, parents, children, and acquaintances; your home is quiet, and all who live there enjoy an excellent sense of relaxation. Upon entering your house, others feel a sense of happiness. When your mind is not peaceful and tamed, not only will you repeatedly get angry, but others, upon entering your door, will immediately sense that a lot of fighting takes place in this house—that this person frequently gets worked up.

Since taming the mind brings happiness and not doing so leads to suffering, use your life to reduce the number of untamed attitudes—such as controlling enemies, promoting friends, increasing monetary profit, and the like—and to tame, or train, your mind as much as possible. This is the way to extract the meaningful essence of this precious and tenuous human body.

SUMMARY ADVICE

1. Realize the value of the human body with which you have been endowed, for it is the result of many past good causes. Appreciate the fact that teachings are available and ready to be implemented.

2. Since this precious human life can be used in powerfully beneficial or destructive ways, and is itself most fragile, make good use of it now.

3. Physical happiness is just an occasional balance of elements in the body, not a deep harmony. Understand the temporary for what it is.

4. A tamed mind makes you peaceful, relaxed, and happy, whereas if your mind is not peaceful and tamed, no matter how wonderful your external circumstances, you will be beset by frights and worries. Realize that the root of your own happiness and welfare rests with a peaceful and tamed mind. It is also a great benefit to those around you.

Stanza Three

May we realize that there is no time to waste,
Death being definite but the time of death indefinite.
What has gathered will separate, what has been
*   accumulated will be consumed without residue,*
At the end of a rising comes descent, the finality of
*   birth is death.*

From beginningless time we have been under the influence of an illusion of permanence, so we think there is always lots of time remaining. This puts us in great danger of wasting our lives in procrastination. To counteract this tendency, it is important to meditate on impermanence, on the fact that death might come at any moment.

Even though there is no certainty you *will* die tonight, when you cultivate an awareness of death, you appreciate that you *could* die tonight. With this attitude, if there is something you can do that will help both this life and the next, you will give it precedence over something that will just help this life in a superficial way. Furthermore, by being uncertain about when death will come, you will refrain from doing something that will harm both your present and your future lifetimes. As this sense of caution develops, you will strive harder not to accumulate unfavorable predispositions through uncontrolled actions. You will be motivated to develop, according to your ability, attitudes that act as antidotes to the various forms of an untamed mind. Then, whether you live a day, a week, a month, or a year, that time will be meaningful; your thoughts and actions will be based on what is beneficial in the long run, and the longer you live the more beneficial they will be.

By contrast, when you come under the influence of the illusion of permanence and spend your time on matters that go no deeper than the surface of this life, you sustain great loss. This is why, in this stanza, the Panchen Lama directs our attention to the value of making each moment count.

In my own case, I am now sixty-seven years old. I am the oldest of the thirteen Dalai Lamas who came before me, except for the First Dalai Lama, Gendun Drup, who lived into his eighties. The Fifth Dalai Lama lived to be sixty-six; I am older than he—I am an old man! Still, because of recent developments in medical treatment and living conditions, I have some hope of staying until eighty or ninety, but it is definite that at some time or other I must die. We Tibetans even think that we can lengthen our lifespan through rituals, but I am not sure whether those who perform these live longer. To perform a long-life ritual it is necessary to have stable visualization within concentrated meditation. In addition, it is necessary to understand the emptiness of inherent existence, since it is wisdom itself that manifests as your imagined, ideal self. Also, it is necessary to have compassion and an altruistic intention to become enlightened. These requirements make long-life meditations difficult.

Since our attitudes of permanence and self-cherishing—held in our hearts as if they were the center of life—are what ruin us, the most fruitful meditations are on impermanence, the emptiness of inherent existence, and compassion. Without these, long-life rituals and the like will not help. This is why Buddha emphasized that the two wings of the bird flying to enlightenment are compassion and wisdom. These two are the ways to oppose attitudes of permanence and self-cherishing, which, since beginningless time, have undermined our aims for happiness.

At around age fifteen or sixteen I studied the stages of the path to enlightenment and began some form of meditation to cultivate the steps. I also began to give teachings during which I had to perform more and more analytical meditation, since teaching and analytical meditation go hand in hand. The topic of the awareness of death is organized around three roots, nine reasons, and three decisions:

First root: Contemplation that death is definite

1. because death will definitely come and therefore cannot be avoided
2. because our lifespan cannot be extended and diminishes unceasingly

3. because even when we are alive there is little time to practice

First decision: I must practice.

Second root: Contemplation that the time of death is indefinite

4. because our lifespan in this world is indefinite
5. because the causes of death are very many and the causes of life are few
6. because the time of death is uncertain due to the fragility of the body

Second decision: I must practice now.

Third root: Contemplation that at the time of death nothing helps except practice

7. because at the time of death our friends are of no help
8. because at the time of death our wealth is of no help
9. because at the time of death our body is of no help

Third decision: I will practice non-attachment to any of the wonderful things of this life.

It is the nature of cyclic existence that what has gathered will eventually disperse—parents, children, brothers, sisters, and friends. No matter how much friends like each other, eventually they must separate. Gurus and students, parents and children, brothers and sisters, husbands and wives, and friends—no matter who they are—must eventually separate.

While my senior tutor, Ling Rinpochay, was healthy, it was almost impossible, unbearable, for me to think about his death. For me, he was always like a very solid rock on which I could rely. I wondered how I could survive without him. But when he suffered a stroke, after which there was a second, very serious stroke, eventually the situation allowed part of my mind to think, "Now it would be better for him to go." Sometimes I have even thought that he deliberately took on that illness, so that when he did actually pass away, I would be ready to handle the next task—to search for his reincarnation.

In addition to separating from all of our friends, the wealth and resources that accumulate over time—no matter how marvelous they are—eventually become unusable. No matter how high your rank or position, you must eventually fall. To remind myself of this, when I ascend the high platform from which I teach, just as I am sitting down, I recite to myself the words of the *Diamond Cutter Sutra* about impermanence:

> View things compounded from causes
> To be like twinkling stars, figments seen with an
>   eye disease,
> The flickering light of a butter lamp, magical
>   illusions,
> Dew, bubbles, dreams, lightning, and clouds.

I reflect on the fragility of caused phenomena, and then snap my fingers, the brief sound symbolizing impermanence. This is how I remind myself that I will soon be descending from the high throne.

Any living being—no matter how long he or she lives—must eventually die. There is no other way. Once you dwell within cyclic existence, you cannot live outside of its nature. No matter how marvelous things may be, it is built into their very nature that they and you, who take joy in them, must degenerate in the end.

Not only must you die in the end, but you do not know when the end will come. If you did, you could put off preparing for the future. Even if you show signs of living to a ripe old age, you cannot say with one hundred percent certainty that today you will not die. You must not procrastinate. Rather, you should make preparations so that even if you did die tonight, you would have no regrets. If you develop an appreciation for the uncertainty and imminence of death, your sense of the importance of using your time wisely will get stronger and stronger. As the Tibetan scholar-yogi Tsongkhapa says:

> When the difficulty of finding this human body
>   is understood, there is no way to stay doing
>   nothing.
> When its great meaning is seen, passing the time
>   senselessly is a cause of sorrow.
> When death is contemplated, preparation to go
>   to the next life is made.
> When actions and their effects are contemplated,
>   sources of non-conscientiousness are turned
>   away.
> When in this way these four roots have become
>   firm,
> Other virtuous practices easily grow.

Thinking about death not only serves as a preparation for dying and prompts actions that benefit future lives, but it also dramatically affects your mental perspective. For instance, when people are not accustomed to this practice of being mindful about the certainty of death, then even when it is obvious that they are old and will soon pass away, their friends and family feel they cannot be realistic with them, and even feel the need to compliment them on their physical appearance. Both parties know it is a lie. It is ridiculous!

Sometimes even patients suffering from terminal diseases such as cancer avoid using the words "die" or "death." I find it almost impossible to speak with them about their impending death; they resist hearing about it. But for one who cannot now face even the word "death," never mind the reality of it, the actual arrival of death is likely to bring with it great discomfort and fear. On the other hand, when I meet with a practitioner who appears to be near death, I do not hesitate to say, "Whether you die or recover, you need preparation for both." It is possible for us to reflect together on the imminence of death. There is no need to hide anything, for that person is prepared to face death with no regret. A practitioner who, early on, thinks about impermanence is much more courageous and happy while dying. Reflecting on the uncertainty of the time of death develops a mind that is peaceful, disciplined, and virtuous, because it is dwelling on more than the superficial stuff of this short lifetime.

SUMMARY ADVICE

1. If you cultivate a sense of the uncertainty of the time of death, you will make better use of your time.
2. To prevent procrastination with regard to spiritual practice, take care not to come under the influence of the illusion of permanence.
3. Realize that no matter how wonderful a situation may be, its nature is such that it must end.
4. Do not think that there will be time later.
5. Be frank about facing your own death. Skillfully encourage others to be frank about their deaths. Do not deceive each other with compliments when the time of death is near. Honesty will foster courage and joy.

4

Removing Obstacles to a Favorable Death

Though you hold fast, you cannot stay.
What benefit is there
In being frightened and scared
Of what is unalterable?

—BUDDHA

Stanza Four

*May we be relieved from overwhelming suffering due to
the various causes of death
When in this city of erroneous conceptions of subject
and object
The illusory body composed of the four impure elements
And consciousness are about to separate.*

Begin as early as possible in your life to gain familiarity with virtuous states of mind. When this capacity is
established, it will be possible to direct the mind toward

virtue even while dying. However, while dying you could be overwhelmed with incapacitating pain from a terrible illness, you may suffer an untimely death in an accident or from an attack, or you may not be able to finish your lifespan due to exhaustion of merit—using up your store of the good karma that keeps this lifetime going. These circumstances could render your long practice with virtuous states of mind unworkable (though this is not necessarily so). Suffering itself could generate so much fright that virtuous contemplation becomes impossible, except for those who have trained to a high degree and have great powers of concentrated meditation. Therefore, it is important to make wishes now to be free from such overwhelming pain and fear, and to die in a relaxed way; this allows the virtuous attitude you have been cultivating to be strong; you will be able to die with greater understanding.

Since death involves the separation of body and mind, it is important to realize the nature of the "I" that is set up relative to the collection of physical and mental aggregates, as well as the nature of those aggregates themselves. The type of body we possess is an impure entity, produced from the four elements of earth, water, fire, and wind, subject to pain from even slight causes, and like an illusion both in the sense of being here one moment and gone the next, and in the sense of appearing to exist inherently but actually being empty of such inherent existence. By appearing to be clean if washed, and appearing blissful, permanent, and under your control, the body dwells, so to speak, in a city of misconceptions about the nature of consciousness and its objects.

The city of erroneous conceptions in the fourth stanza refers to cyclic existence. It is built by actions (karma) that are under the influence of afflictive emotions. Afflictive emotions arise from ignorance, specifically the conception of inherent existence, which mistakes the nature of self and other, as well as things, conceiving these to exist by way of their own being. Therefore, ignorance is the fundamental cause of the painful round and round of cyclic existence.

The false apprehension of inherent existence motivates karma—both actions and the predispositions accumulated from those actions—the driver of cyclic existence. The phenomena that arise due to this process of ignorance appear to exist inherently, but they do not, and thus are a city of mistakenness. The city of cyclic existence is created by the misconception that subject and object, apprehender and apprehended, internal and external phenomena, exist in and of themselves, inherently, under their own power.

With this stanza you are making the wish that when consciousness is about to separate from the illusory body composed of the four elements, you will not be afflicted with overwhelming suffering, since this would interfere with successful practice. Other conditions preventing practice are lust and hatred, which are huge obstacles to a virtuous attitude.

SUMMARY ADVICE

1. Practice now so that at the time of death the force of your familiarity with virtue will affect your attitude.

2. View the body as a veritable city of misconceptions, because though it appears to be clean when you wash it, as well as a source of bliss, permanent, and under your control, it is not. It is produced from the four elements (earth, water, fire, and wind), is subject to pain, and changes from moment to moment of its own accord.

3. People and things appear to exist under their own

power, and ignorance accepts this false appearance, giving rise to the afflictive emotions of lust, hatred, and more bewilderment. These afflictive emotions in turn pollute actions of body, speech, and mind, perpetuating the process of cyclic existence. Understand that you live in a city of misconceptions.

Stanza Five

May we be relieved from mistaken appearances of
    nonvirtue
When, deceived at the time of need by this body
    sustained so dearly,
The frightful enemies—the lords of death—manifest
And we kill ourselves with the weapons of the three
    poisons of lust, hatred, and bewilderment.

The time of death is very important, for it marks the end of one life and the beginning of another. If at this crucial time your body remained with you, you could put your trust in it, but at this important time it deceives you. Your body, sustained so dearly with food, clothing, money, shelter, medicine, and even ill deeds, abandons you.

Just the mention of death makes us a little uncomfortable. When the process of your own death becomes manifest and the frightful aspects of impermanence, called "lords of death" in the poem, show themselves, some people respond with strong attachment to their possessions, relatives, friends, and body, while others evince hatred for their enemies and for their seemingly unbearable suffering. Even if lust and hatred are not present, you generate a strong belief in your own inherent existence and that of all appearances—the central form of ignorance. These three poisons—lust, hatred, and ignorance—are the strongest internal obstacles to virtuous practice, and in a deeper sense, these are the weapons with which you kill yourself at death. To keep these poisonous attitudes from arising while dying, plant wishes that strong lust and hatred should not arise and that false appearances should not occur.

At death it is important to be free from medicines that would make you unable to think properly. For a religious practitioner mind-dulling drugs are to be avoided, since your mental consciousness must be as clear as possible. Taking an injection to allow a "peaceful death" could deprive the mind of the opportunity of manifesting in a virtuous way by reflecting on impermanence, generating faith, feeling compassion, or meditating on selflessness. However, if a pain-killing drug that does not dull the mind is developed, it could even be useful, since you could continue your usual mental functioning, free from the distraction of pain.

SUMMARY ADVICE

1. Understand that this body, which you sustain at any cost, will someday desert you.
2. Avoid lusting after the situation you are leaving.
3. Avoid hating that you have to leave.
4. Keep away from lust, hatred, and ignorance as much as possible so that you can maintain virtuous practice while dying.
5. Realize that by taking a pill or an injection to have a so-called peaceful death you may be depriving yourself of a crucial opportunity for manifesting virtue.

5

Gaining Favorable Conditions
for the Time of Death

Some die in the womb,
Others at birth,
Still others when they can crawl,
Some when they can walk.

Some are old,
Others are adults,
Going one by one
Like fruit falling to the ground.
—BUDDHA

Stanza Six
May we remember instructions for practice
When doctors forsake us and rites are of no avail,
Friends have given up hope for our life,
And we are left with nothing else to do.

The previous chapter was mainly concerned with
two obstacles to proper practice when dying—over-

whelming suffering and mistaken appearances that give rise to lust, hatred, or confusion. While seeking to avoid these two obstacles, you also need to generate virtuous attitudes by remembering your practice. When there is no longer any hope for this life, when doctors have given up on you, when religious rites are no longer of any avail, and when even your friends and relatives have from the depths given up hope, you must do what helps. As long as you have mindfulness, you must do whatever you can to keep the mind in a virtuous way.

To do this you will need to remember instructions for generating virtuous attitudes. As I will discuss in later stanzas, these instructions are to be used (1) before the clear light of death; (2) when the clear light of death manifests; (3) when the clear light of death ceases and the intermediate state begins; and (4) during the intermediate state so you can achieve special yogic feats. Whatever instructions you have received in accordance with your ability and intelligence need to be remembered clearly at these times. Conduct your usual practice at whatever level you have attained during these times.

Through the following five forces your practice can have great effect:

1. *The force of familiarity.* Frequently cultivate and become accustomed to whatever your usual practice is—whether this is cultivation of the intention to be liberated from cyclic existence, cultivation of love and compassion, cultivation of an intention to gain enlightenment for the good of others, or cultivation of the stages of Highest Yoga Tantra.

2. *The force of directing the future.* Think, "I will maintain my practice in this life, the intermediate state, and future lives until I attain Buddhahood."

3. *The force of wholesome seeds.* Amass the force of meritorious actions (good karma) to propel your practice.

4. *The force of eradication.* Decide that all phenomena such as birth, death, and intermediate state exist only dependently—they do not have inherent existence, even in the slightest. Make this decision as part of your belief that self-cherishing is an enemy, thinking, "That I experience suffering in cyclic existence is due to self-cherishing; the root of self-cherishing comes from conceiving that beings and things inherently exist, whereas they do not."

5. *The force of wishing.* Again and again make the following wish: "Even after dying may I attain a body

that serves as a support for practicing the doctrine in my next life. Being cared for by an excellent spiritual guide, may I not be separated from practice."

These five forces are especially helpful in remembering to practice, even when it is hardest to do so.

When it is clear that someone is about to die, friends should *not* gather around the person in an attached way, grasping at the dying person's hand, tearfully embracing him or her, or bemoaning the situation. This will not help at all; instead, such behavior serves to generate a desirous attitude in the dying person's mind, ruining any chance of generating a virtuous one. Friends should help provide the right conditions for generation of virtue by reminding the person of religious instructions and practices, speaking gently into the ear until the external breath ceases.

For instance, if the dying person believes in a creator God, then thinking of God may make the person more comfortable, more peaceful, and have less attachment, fear, and regret. If the person believes in rebirth, then thinking about a meaningful next life in the service of others will have similar results. A Buddhist could be mindful of Buddha and dedicate good deeds in this life toward a productive new life. A nonbeliever could similarly reflect that death is an integral part of life, and now that it is happening there is no use to worry. The main point is peace of mind in order not to disturb the process of death.

SUMMARY ADVICE

1. It is helpful to know that at some point all hope for continuing this life will end. At that point doctors, priests, friends, and relatives cannot keep you in this life; it will be up to you to do what helps.

2. While dying, you need to remember spiritual instructions that accord with your own level of practice and enact them.

3. Develop familiarity with your practice. Be determined to maintain this spiritual direction in all situations, no matter how difficult. Engage in many meritorious actions so that their accumulated force affects all aspects of your life and death. Realize that suffering arises from self-cherishing and learn to cherish others. Frequently wish to maintain your spiritual practice through future lives.

4. When another person dies, be careful not to upset him or her by causing more attachment or stirring up anger and hatred. Do not bemoan their departure, grasp at them, or cry in their presence. Help them to depart meaningfully by reminding them of deeper practice.

5. If it is at all possible, ask others to do the same for you. Arrange to have someone near you who will speak softly into your ear from time to time, reminding you of a specific spiritual attitude that you want to manifest.

Stanza Seven

May we have the confidence of joy and delight
When food and wealth accumulated with miserliness are
    left behind
And we separate forever from cherished and longed-for
    friends,
Going alone to a perilous situation.

Ordinarily, if you were told that your death was imminent, it would be sorrowful, not only for yourself but for friends and family. Within this sorrow, the process of dying—the gradual withdrawal of consciousness—would take place. However, if, as explained above, you have reflected on the importance of extracting the essence of this life situation and the necessity for spiritual practice, and have reflected again and again on impermanence, then through remembering these instructions while dying, you will not come under the influence of unfavorable conditions such as grief and sorrow. All of the appearances associated with death, instead of distracting you, remind you of the practice and urge you toward meditation.

With this in mind, it will be possible to die with joy and confidence, like a child happily returning to her parents' home. Among those who will go into an intermediate state between lives, the best can determine their next birth; such a person can die with confidence, without any worry. A middling practitioner will not be frightened, and the lowest at least will not have any regret. Since you have prepared for being reborn in a meaningful way—being able to continue spiritual endeavor—there is no regret, depression, or fright when death comes. Your consciousness can leave with great confidence.

A number of monastics and scholars that I know

have died in such a way. They realized they were about to die and called in their close acquaintances to bid them farewell. On the day of their deaths they put on their saffron monastic robes, and without the slightest worry died in meditation. A monk here in Dharmsala, after asking one of his helpers to bring him his robe, put it on and passed away. Several here in India have been able to stay within the mind of clear light for many days—one for seventeen, others for nine or ten. As a sign of this, after their breathing stopped, their bodies remained completely fresh, without the slightest foul odor, for all that time in this hot country. Such persons are able to remain without fluctuation in the mind of clear light of death, and die with tremendous confidence and joy.

My senior tutor, Ling Rinpochay, told me a story about a lama that is both sad and funny at the same time. Near the time of his death, the lama put on his saffron robe and told his companions that he was about to die. Then, while sitting in the cross-legged posture of meditation, he died. One of his new students, who, having recently arrived from an outlying area, did not know about the possibility of dying within sitting meditation, came into the lama's room and saw that his teacher's body was sitting up. He imagined that a spirit had entered the body of his teacher; so he knocked the body down!

SUMMARY ADVICE

1. To avoid being depressed about dying, take refuge in your respective religion within compassion for all beings; reflect on the importance of extracting the essence of this present life, which is endowed with both the leisure and the necessities of spiritual practice, and reflect again and again on impermanence.

2. With that groundwork for effectively remembering your practice while dying, even horrific events and appearances that might occur will only serve to urge you to be calm and to meditate with joy and confidence.

6

Meditating While Dying

This life disappears only very quickly
Like something written in water with a stick.

—BUDDHA

Stanza Eight

May we generate a powerful mind of virtue
When the elements—earth, water, fire, and wind—
  dissolve in stages
And physical strength is lost, mouth and nose dry and
  pucker,
Warmth withdraws, breaths are gasped, and rattling
  sounds emerge.

The first seven stanzas are presented in accordance
with both forms of Buddhist doctrine, Sutra and Tantra;
the latter involves a special practice that calls for imagining yourself here and now as a fully compassionate

and wise being with the physical form of a Buddha. From the eighth stanza on, the presentation is mainly of Tantra practices, specifically from the class of Highest Yoga Tantra.

The description of death in terms of the gradual dissolution of body and mind and of the four elements is unique to Highest Yoga Tantra. After conception a process of formation proceeds from subtler to grosser, but at death there is a dissolution from grosser to subtler. The phenomena that dissolve consist of the four elements—earth (the hard substance of the body), water (fluids), fire (heat), and wind (energy, movement).

Whether you live out your full lifespan or not, the process of death involves many phases. In a sudden death you pass through these phases very quickly, with little chance of noticing them; for those who die more gradually, it is possible to recognize and make use of these different stages. Portents of death, such as a change in the way the breath moves in the nostrils, dreams, and physical signs, can occur even many years before actual death, though for ordinary persons these usually occur within a year or two before dying. Portents of death include becoming disgusted with your surroundings, home, friends, and so forth, resulting in a wish to go elsewhere. Or, you may develop lust for these exceeding what you had before. You may switch from being harsh to being cooperative, or the other way around. Your enthusiasm might markedly increase or wane. There may be a change in your physical luster or the style of your behavior. The nature of your conversation may become very rough—swearing and so forth—or you might talk repeatedly about death.

When the actual process of dying begins, you pass through eight phases. The first four involve the collapse of the four elements. The last four involve the collapse of consciousness into the innermost level of mind, called the mind of clear light. Remember, the presentation of the phases of death is a mapping of deeper states of mind that occur throughout daily life and usually go unnoticed. These eight phases proceed in forward order when dying, going to sleep, ending a dream, sneezing, fainting, and during orgasm, and in reverse order after the process of death completely ends, as well as when waking from sleep, when beginning a dream, and when sneezing, fainting, and orgasm end.

The eight stages are identified by way of visual content although not seen with the eyes:

Forward Order

1. mirage
2. smoke
3. fireflies
4. flame of a lamp
5. vivid white mind-sky
6. vivid red-orange mind-sky
7. vivid black mind-sky
8. clear light

Reverse Order

1. clear light
2. vivid black mind-sky
3. vivid red-orange mind-sky
4. vivid white mind-sky
5. flame of a lamp
6. fireflies
7. smoke
8. mirage

THE FIRST FOUR PHASES IN THE FORWARD ORDER: THE COLLAPSE OF THE FOUR ELEMENTS

In general, the grosser elements dissolve into the subtler. As the capacity of the former to serve as a support for consciousness degenerates, the latter becomes more manifest. There are eight phases, the first four of which are:

Phase 1. The earth element degenerates and dissolves into the water element. The solid aspects of the body, such as bone, are no longer capable of serving as a mount, or foundation, for consciousness; the capacity of the solid aspects to do so dissolves into, or is transferred to, the fluids of the body, such as blood and phlegm. Now the capacity of the water element to act as a base of consciousness becomes more manifest. Your body becomes dramatically thinner and your limbs loosen. You lose physical strength—the vitality and luster of the body radically diminishes, leaving it worn out. Your sight becomes dark and unclear; you can no longer open and close your eyes. You may have a sense of sinking into the earth or under mud, and you may even call out, "Hold me up!" or attempt to struggle upward, but it is important not to fight; remain calm within a virtuous attitude. What you see in your mind looks like a mirage.

Phase 2. The capacity of the water element degenerates and dissolves into the fire element—the warmth that maintains the body—and the fire element's capacity to serve as a basis of consciousness is enhanced. You no longer experience feelings of pleasure and pain, or even neutral feelings, associated with the senses and the mental consciousness. Your mouth, tongue, and throat dry due to loss of saliva, and scum forms on the teeth. Other fluids, such as urine, blood, regenerative fluid, and sweat, dry up. You can no longer hear sounds, and the usual hum in the ears stops. What you see in your mind looks like puffs of smoke, or thin smoke throughout a room, or smoke billowing from a chimney.

Phase 3. The capacity of the fire element degenerates and dissolves into the wind element—the currents of air, or energy, that direct various bodily functions such as inhalation, exhalation, burping, spitting, speaking, swallowing, flexing the joints, stretching and contracting the limbs, opening and closing the mouth and eyelids, digestion, urination, defecation, menstruation, and ejaculation. The warmth of the body diminishes, resulting in an inability to digest food. If you have conducted your life predominantly without virtue, the bodily warmth initially gathers downward from the top of the head to the heart, the upper body becoming cold first; but if you have lived predominantly virtuously, warmth gathers from the soles of the feet upward to the heart, and the lower body becomes cold first. The ability to smell ceases. You can no longer pay attention to the activities and wishes of friends and relatives around you, or even remember their names. You experience difficulty breathing, exhalations becoming longer and longer and inhalations shorter and shorter; your throat emits rattling or gasping sounds. What you see in your mind looks like fireflies, perhaps inside smoke, or like sparks in the soot on the bottom of a metal pan.

Phase 4. The capacity of the coarser wind element degenerates and dissolves into consciousness. The tongue becomes thick and short, its root turning bluish. Experiencing physical touch is impossible, as is physical action. The breath through the nostrils ceases, but there are subtler levels of breath, or wind, so the cessation of breath through the nose does not indicate the completion of the death process. What you see in your mind is like the flame of a butter lamp or a candle (or like the flickering light *above* a butter lamp or candle). At first the light flickers as if the butter or wax were almost consumed. Then, when the winds on which mental conceptions ride begin to collapse, the flame's appearance becomes steady.

In general, the body of a human is composed of the four elements; however, due to variations in the channels and winds within this framework, different people experience different internal appearances during the process of dissolution. This is why there are small variations in the explanations of this process in specific Tantras spoken by Buddha, such as *Guhyasamaja* (the main system being explained in this book), *Chakrasamvara,* and *Kalachakra,* as well as in certain Tantras of the Old Translation Order of Tibetan Buddhism, called Nyingma. These minor variations mainly come from differences in the channels within the body and in winds and drops of essential fluid that course through those channels. Because these internal factors differ in individuals, yoga practices also differ slightly. Even when internal factors are the same, the internal signs of dying appear to the mind in different ways because yogis put emphasis on different points in the body.

During these stages you need an unobstructed virtuous attitude, which is the wish expressed in this stanza of the Panchen Lama's poem. We ordinary sentient beings under the influence of birth and death definitely have predispositions established over lifetimes of good and bad actions, the fruits of which have not yet manifested. Every moment that we engage in actions motivated by ignorance contributes to living in cyclic existence. Very strong actions can propel not just one but many lives in cyclic existence. Near the time of death, one of these many wholesome and unwholesome karmic predispositions is nourished and serves as the foundation for the whole next lifetime; many other karmas establish the qualities of life such as health, resources, and intelligence. Consequently, your thoughts, your mental state, near the time of death are very important.

Even if most of your life you practiced virtuous attitudes, a strong nonvirtuous tendency near the time of death can nourish the nonvirtuous predispositions we all have; this is a very dangerous time. Even from an annoying noise made by someone's setting down an object too hard, irritation and anger can develop. Conversely, a person not usually accustomed to much virtue can generate a strong virtuous mind near death, activating karmic predispositions for virtue and resulting in a good rebirth. Therefore, you must take great care near the time of death and generate, as much as possible, whatever type of virtuous attitude you are capable of manifesting. It is very important that those attending the dying know that the dying person's mind is in a delicate state; they should be careful not to make disturbances—speaking loudly, crying, and roughly handling articles—and, instead, create a peaceful environment.

SUMMARY ADVICE

1. So that you will not be surprised by the dying process when it starts, learn the stages of the dissolution of the four elements and their accompanying external signs, as given above, and the internal signs, described in the following stanza.

2. Take care near the time of death so that good predispositions are nourished and activated by virtuous attitudes.

3. Portents of death can appear within a year or two prior to dying. These alert you to the need to prepare, but it is better to be ready before then.

Stanza Nine

May we realize the deathless mode of being
When various mistaken appearances frightful and
  horrible
And in particular mirage, smoke, and fireflies appear
And the mounts of the eighty indicative conceptions
  cease.

When the four elements dissolve, various appearances occur. Sometimes even before the eye and ear cease to function, unusual sights and sounds appear. And always, various visions appear to the mental consciousness. For example, some who have suffered from a debilitating disease might see terrible fire, creating great fear. Others experience pleasant and even amazing visions and remain relaxed. Differences like these come from predispositions established by nonvirtuous and virtuous actions in this and previous lives. These differences signal the type and quality of the rebirth about to occur, the way the quality of light in the sky before sunrise foretells the day's weather.

As the four elements dissolve one by one, the internal signs of death appear. The dissolution of the earth element into water produces an appearance like a mirage on a desert; the dissolution of water into fire results in an appearance like puffs of smoke from a chimney or thin smoke spread throughout a room; the dissolution of fire into wind creates an appearance like fireflies, or like sparks in the soot on the bottom of a wok that is used to parch grain. (The dissolution of the wind element will be discussed in the next chapter.)

Those signs—mirage, smoke, fireflies, and flame as well as the four to be described below—appear to those who die gradually. They do not occur in complete form to those who die suddenly, killed in accidents or by weapons.

SUMMARY ADVICE

1. Realize that the myriad appearances, some even frightening and horrible, which might occur while dying are due to karma. Do not be distracted by them.

2. Learn the first three of the eight appearances: mirage like that in a desert; puffs of smoke from a chimney or thin smoke throughout a room; fireflies, or sparks in the soot on the bottom of a wok.

Stanza Ten

May we generate strong mindfulness and introspection
When the wind constituent begins to dissolve into
   consciousness
And the external continuum of breath ceases, coarse
   dualistic appearances dissolve,
And an appearance like a burning butter lamp dawns.

Consciousness is defined as that which is luminous and knowing. It is luminous in the double sense that its nature is clear and that it illuminates, or reveals, like a lamp that dispels darkness so that objects may be seen. Consciousness also knows objects in the sense that it at least apprehends them, even when it does not know them properly.

Consciousness is composed of moments, instead of cells, atoms, or particles. In this way consciousness and matter have basically different natures, and therefore, they have different substantial causes. Material things have other material things as their substantial causes (so called since they produce the substance, or basic entity, of the effect), because there must be an agreement in basic nature between substantial cause and substantial effect. Clay, for example, is the substantial cause of a clay pot. The substantial cause of a mind must itself be something that is luminous and knowing—a previous moment of mind. Any moment of consciousness, therefore, requires a preceding moment of consciousness for its substantial cause, which means that there must be a beginningless continuum of mind. This is how a beginningless round of rebirth is established through reasoning. In addition, if there is one accurate memory of rebirth, that is a sufficient indication—not everyone has to remember. The absence of former and future lives has never been directly perceived, whereas there are attested cases of clear memory of former lives. Despite the fact that the body depends on conditions for its increase and decrease, the body is endowed with life, and when that life force ceases, it quickly rots and becomes a corpse. No matter how beautiful or handsome it has been, it turns into a corpse. If you analyze this life force that keeps the body from rotting, you will see that it is the mind. The fact that flesh is conjoined with consciousness keeps it from decomposing. The continuum of this mind is what proceeds to the next lifetime.

The difference in nature between mind and matter requires that their substantial causes be different, but this does not mean that mind and matter do not interact, for they do so in many ways. Matter can be a cooperative condition of mind, such as when the subtle matter inside the orb of the eye acts as a cooperative condition of visual consciousness, or when a color or shape acts as a cooperative condition of visual consciousness, or when your own body acts as a support, or base, of consciousness itself.

Similarly, consciousness shapes matter since it is our actions, or karmas, motivated by consciousness, that structure the environment. The pooled influence of the karmas of many beings shape the very world-system we inhabit. Also, according to Highest Yoga Tantra, consciousness rides on wind that is physical, though in its subtlest forms wind is not composed of particles. Because of this close association between mind and wind such that they are one undifferentiable entity, an enlightened being can manifest a body with subtle wind as its substantial cause, a body beyond physical particles, as in the case of a Buddha's Complete Enjoyment Body in a Pure Land.

Applying this doctrine of substantial causes and cooperative conditions to conception, we can see that the substances of mother and father—ovum and sperm—act as the substantial causes of the body of the child and act as cooperating conditions of the mind. The last moment of that child's consciousness in its previous life acts as the substantial cause of consciousness at the moment of conception and as a cooperating condition of the body. Just as on a coarse level the body—even the embryo—is considered to be the physical support of consciousness, so the wind on which consciousness is mounted, like a rider on a horse, is a physical entity that supports consciousness. Although consciousness can separate from the physical body, as it does when we pass from one lifetime to another, consciousness can never separate from the subtlest level of wind.

I do not think that the very subtle wind, or energy, can be classified as one of the four elements—earth, water, fire, and wind—since it is beyond physical particles. The very subtle wind is one aspect of the movement of very subtle mind; it is the same entity as its respective mind. It would be difficult to analyze very subtle wind and mind with scientific instruments; however, it might be possible to scientifically detect the presence of very subtle wind and mind in cases of clinical death before the exit of consciousness from the body while the body has still not decomposed. A few scientists brought some machines to our hospital, but while they were here, no one died, and then when spiritually experienced persons died, the machines were not available!

When wind, or the energy on which the various levels of consciousness ride, becomes very weak and dissolves more fully into consciousness, subtler and subtler levels of mind manifest. At the beginning of the fourth phase, when the winds that serve as the mounts of the many attitudes begin to dissolve, there appears to the mind an image like the flame of a butter lamp or of a candle, flickering at first and then steady. The outer breath ceases. The world generally considers this to be the moment of death though it is actually later. At this stage, grosser levels of the appearance of subject and object as distant and cut off into separate entities dissolve; the eye does not see visible forms, the ear does not hear sounds, the nose does not smell odors, the tongue does not experience tastes, and the body does not feel tangible objects. The luminous and knowing nature of the mind emerges nakedly.

If you are able to be mindful at death, recognizing the signs of the stages of dissolution, maintaining introspection enough to strive at whatever level of virtue you know, your practice will be very powerful. At the very least, it will positively affect your next life.

SUMMARY ADVICE

1. Although mind and matter have different substantial causes, they interact in many ways.
2. After the three internal signs of mirage, smoke, and fireflies, comes the fourth internal sign, which is like the flame of a butter lamp or of a candle, at first flickering and then steady.
3. Although at this point the outer breath through the nose ceases and there is no conscious reaction to external stimuli, the person has not died. It is helpful if the body is not disturbed until full death occurs.
4. Maintaining mindfulness and introspection that help you recognize which phase of the internal process is occurring can impel powerful realization and influence a positive rebirth.

7

The Inner Structure

A tomorrow when you are gone
Is undoubtedly coming.
—SHURA'S *LETTER TO KANIKA*

Stanza Eleven
May we know our own nature ourselves
Through the yoga realizing cyclic existence and nirvana
  as empty
When appearance, increase, and near-attainment
  dissolve—the earlier into the later—
And experiences like pervasive moonlight, sunlight, and
  darkness dawn.

To get a picture of the final four phases of the death process, it is essential to understand the levels of consciousness as well as the structure of channels, winds, and drops of essential fluid inside the body. This is important Tantra physiology and psychology.

LEVELS OF CONSCIOUSNESS

Highest Yoga Tantra divides consciousness into gross, subtle, and very subtle levels. The *gross levels* include the five sense consciousnesses—the eye consciousness that apprehends colors and shapes; the ear consciousness for sounds; the nose consciousness for odors; the tongue consciousness for tastes; the body consciousness for tactile experience. These are individual consciousnesses with specific spheres of activity—colors and shapes, sounds, odors, tastes, and tactile experience.

More subtle than these but still on the gross level is the consciousness with which we think. It is grouped into three classes, corresponding to three types of wind—strong, middling, and weak—on which the three classes of consciousness ride. The first group involves a strong movement of wind to its objects and includes thirty-three conceptual experiences, such as fear, attachment, hunger, thirst, compassion, acquisitiveness, and jealousy. The second group is composed of conceptual consciousnesses that involve a medium movement of wind to their objects—forty conceptions, such as joy, amazement, generosity, desiring to kiss, heroism, non-gentleness, and crookedness. The third group involves a weak movement of wind to its objects—seven conceptions, which are forgetfulness, mistakenness as in apprehending water in a mirage, catatonia, depression, laziness, doubt, and equal desire and hatred. (Within each of those three groups of consciousnesses, or conceptions, there are levels of grossness and subtlety.)

These three categories of conceptual experiences fall within the gross level of mind but they are subtler than the five sense consciousnesses. They are reflections, so to speak, of deeper levels of consciousness that have less and less dualistic perception. They are imprints of three subtle levels of mind that manifest at periods when the grosser levels of consciousness cease, either intentionally—as in profound states of meditation—or naturally, as in the process of death or going to sleep.

When the winds on which all eighty of these conceptions ride collapse, the conceptions also dissolve. This allows three *subtle levels* of consciousness to manifest in this order: minds of vivid white appearance, vivid red-orange appearance, and vivid black appearance.

(These are described below in phases five through seven.) These lead finally to the *very subtle level* of consciousness, the mind of clear light, which, if utilized in the spiritual path, is most powerful. (It is described below in phase eight.)

Before we discuss these final four phases in detail, we must explain the changes on which they depend. In the physiology of Highest Yoga Tantra, these take place in physical channels, winds, and essential drops that course in these channels.

STRUCTURE OF THE CHANNELS IN THE BODY

In the body there are at least seventy-two thousand channels—arteries, veins, ducts, nerves, and manifest and unmanifest pathways—which start growing at what will be the heart soon after conception. The three most important channels run from the point between the eyebrows up to the crown of the head, then down along the front of the backbone to the base of the spine, finally extending to the end of the sexual organ. This description is a way to imagine the central, right, and left channels in meditation, which differs somewhat from where they are in actuality, but imagining them in this ideal way is nevertheless effective in inducing the subtler levels of mind. Sometimes physical descriptions like this merely indicate points of focus to be used in meditation.

At vital places in these three channels are seven channel-wheels, with differing numbers of spokes, or channel-petals:

1. *The wheel of great bliss* resides inside the top of the head, with thirty-two channel-petals. It is called the wheel of great bliss because at its center is the drop of white essential physical fluid that is the foundation of bliss.

2. *The wheel of enjoyment* dwells in the middle of the throat, with sixteen channel-petals. It is called the wheel of enjoyment because this is where tastes are experienced.

3. *The wheel of phenomena* is found at the heart, with eight channel-petals. It is called the wheel of phenomena because it is the residence of the very subtle wind and mind that are themselves the root of all phenomena.

4. *The wheel of emanation* is located at the solar plexus, with sixty-four channel-petals. It is called the wheel of emanation because the inner fire, ignited by yoga training and the means of generating great bliss, dwells there.

5. *The wheel of sustaining bliss* is at the base of the spine, with thirty-two channel-petals. It is called the wheel of sustaining bliss because the deepest level of bliss is sustained from the base of the spine.

6. *The wheel in the middle of the jewel* (the tip of the sexual organ) has sixteen channel-petals.

7. There is also a *wheel between the brows,* with sixteen channel-petals.

At the heart, the right and left channels wrap around the central channel three times (each channel also looping over itself), and then proceed downward. This results in a six-fold constriction at the heart, which prevents the passage of wind in the central channel. Since this constriction is severe, the heart is a dangerous focus of meditation, which could result in nervous breakdown if proper techniques of meditation are not utilized.

At each of these centers—the brow, the top of the head, the throat, the heart, the solar plexus, the base of

the spine, and the sexual organ—the right and left channels wrap around the central channel once each (each
channel also looping over itself), thereby making two
constrictions. The right and left channels are inflated
with wind and constrict the central channel such that
wind cannot move in it; these constrictions are called
"knots." Again, it is important to remember that draw-
ings and descriptions of the structure of the channels
and channel-wheels are meant for practice; they are not
necessarily depictions of their actual shape and posi-
tioning, which can vary greatly from person to person.

STRUCTURE OF THE WINDS
IN THE BODY

When the mind pays attention to an object, it does so
through the movement of wind, or energy. The mind
rides on wind like a rider on a horse. According to
Highest Yoga Tantra, our psycho-physical structure
involves five primary and five secondary winds:

1. *Life-bearing wind.* Its main seat is in the set of channels
   at the heart, and its function is to maintain life. It

also gives rise to the five secondary winds, which govern sensory operation and attention.

2. *Downward-voiding wind.* Its main seat is in the set of channels in the lower abdomen, and it moves about in the womb or the seminal vesicle, in the urinary bladder, in the thighs, and so forth. It stops and starts urination, defecation, and menstruation.

3. *Fire-dwelling wind.* Its main seat is in the set of channels in the solar plexus, where inner heat is generated through yoga. This wind causes digestion, separating refined and unrefined parts, and so forth.

4. *Upward-moving wind.* Its main seat is in the set of channels in the throat. Operating throughout the throat and mouth, this wind causes speech, the tasting of food, swallowing, burping, spitting, and so forth.

5. *Pervasive wind.* Its main seat is in the joints, causing limber movement, stretching and contracting the limbs, and opening and closing the mouth and eyelids.

As you can see, wind drives physical and mental functions. Good health requires free movement of the winds; blockage causes problems.

Ordinarily, wind does not move in the central channel, except during the process of dying; however, through profound yoga techniques, it can—allowing the more profound states of mind to manifest. During the last four phases of dying, the winds that serve as the foundations of consciousness enter into the right and left channels and dissolve there. In turn, the winds in the right and left channels enter into and dissolve in the central channel. The deflation of the right and left channels loosens the constrictions at the channel knots: When the right and left channels become deflated, the central channel is freed, thereby allowing movement of wind inside it. This movement induces the manifestation of subtle minds, which yogis of Highest Yoga Tantra seek to use in the spiritual path; the winds on which a deeply blissful mind rides are intensely withdrawn from moving to objects, and such a mind is particularly powerful in realizing reality.

More than twenty years ago there was a nun over eighty years old who, for her shelter, lived on the veranda of a house in a nearby village. People used to request divinations from her. She asked for an audience, and I met her. She presented me with a book from the Nyingma tradition on practices, called Breakthrough and Leap-Over, and we engaged in casual conversation. She told me that when she was young and still in Tibet, she married, but her husband died, after which she gave up all worldly life, left behind all of her property, and went on a pilgrimage. She eventually reached Drikung, where she met a very old lama, already around eighty, up in a mountain behind Drikung. The lama had around twelve disciples. She reported that on two different occasions she saw monks using their shawls like wings to fly from one hilltop to another. She actually saw this.

If that is true, this is not just a magical feat but comes from practicing wind-yoga. The monks, living in that remote area with an old lama, were clearly renunciates and must have loosened the channel-knots. It seems to me that they must also have had the view of the emptiness of inherent existence, as well as altruism endowed with love and compassion. Whether they were scholars or not, they would have had the essence of understanding emptiness.

DROPS OF ESSENTIAL FLUIDS
IN THE BODY

At the center of the channel-wheels are drops, white on the top and red on the bottom, upon which physical and mental health are based. At the top of the head, the white element predominates, whereas at the solar plexus the red element predominates. These drops originate from the most basic drop at the heart, which is the size of a large mustard seed or small pea, and, like the others, has a white top and red bottom. Since it lasts until death, this drop at the heart is called the "indestructible drop." The very subtle life-bearing wind dwells inside this drop; at death, all winds ultimately dissolve into it, at which point the clear light of death dawns.

Now, with this information about the levels of consciousness, channels, and drops of essential fluids as background, let us return to look at how the levels of consciousness dissolve in the final stages of dying.

UNFOLDING OF THE FINAL FOUR
PHASES OF DEATH

The final four phases of death begin with three levels of subtle mind and conclude with one phase of very subtle mind. The gross levels of consciousness having ceased, three phases of subtle mind emerge. As you proceed through these three levels, your consciousness becomes increasingly non-dualistic, since there is less and less sense of subject and object.

Phase 5. When all eighty conceptions of the gross level of consciousness dissolve, the first of three subtler levels of mind emerges, a vivid white appearance that dawns of its own accord. This is a luminous openness, like an autumn sky suffused by white light. Nothing else appears to this mind. Buddhist tradition uses the example of an autumn sky because in autumn in India, where this teaching originated, the monsoon rains of summer have stopped, leaving the sky clear of clouds and clear of dust. Much in the same way that the sky, or space, is the mere absence of obstruction, coarse conceptions have disappeared, leaving a sense of openness. The first of the three subtler states is called "appearance," because an appearance *like* moonlight dawns, but there is no such light shining from outside. This state is also called "empty," because it is beyond the eighty conceptions and the winds on which they ride.

On a physical level, although it takes place outside what the dying person is experiencing, this is what happens in the fifth phase: (1) The winds in the right and left channels *above* the heart enter the central channel through its opening at the top of the head. (2) Due to this, the knot of channels at the top of the head is loosened. (3) This, in turn, causes the white drop that dwells at the top of the head and has the nature of water to move downward; when it arrives at the top of the sixfold knot of right and left channels at the heart, the vivid white appearance dawns.

Phase 6. When the mind of white appearance and its wind dissolve into the mind of increase-of-appearance, a vivid red-orange appearance dawns of its own accord. This is an even brighter openness, like an autumn sky free from dust and clouds pervaded by red-orange light. Nothing else appears to this mind. This state is called "increase-of-appearance" because an appearance *like* very vivid sunlight appears, but again there is no such light shining from outside. This state is also called "very empty," because it is beyond the mind of appearance and the wind on which it rides.

Physically: (1) The winds in the right and left channels *below* the heart enter the central channel through its lower opening at the base of the spine or sexual organ. (2) Due to this, the knots of the channel-wheels in the sexual organ and at the navel loosen. (3) This causes the red drop (shaped like a small vertical line) in the middle of the channel-wheel at the navel to move upward. As it moves to just below the knot of the right and left channels at the heart, the red-orange increase-of-appearance dawns.

Phase 7. When the mind of red-orange increase-of-appearance and its wind dissolve into the mind of near-attainment, a vivid black appearance dawns of its own accord. Now it is like an autumn sky free from dust and clouds and pervaded by the thick darkness that falls right after dusk. Nothing else appears to this mind. During the first part of the mind of black near-attainment, you are still aware, but in the latter part you become unconscious in a very thick darkness like fainting. This phase is called "near-attainment" because it is close to manifestation of the mind of clear light. It is also called "greatly empty," because it is beyond the mind of increase-of-appearance and the wind on which it rides.

Physically: (1) The upper and lower winds inside the central channel gather at the heart, loosening the six-fold knot of the right and left channels. (2) At this point, the white drop originating at the top of the head further descends, and the red drop originating at the navel further ascends, with both entering into the middle of the indestructible drop at the heart. (3) When these two meet, the vivid black appearance dawns.

Phase 8. The mind becomes even more subtle than it is during the unconscious second part of the mind of black near-attainment; the movement of wind becomes weaker, and the state of the subtlest wind arrives. At this point, unconsciousness is cleared away, and the mind of clear light, the subtlest of all minds, nonconceptual and totally nondualistic, is manifest. At this juncture all conceptual activity has ceased and the three "polluting conditions"—the white, red, and black appearances, or moon, sun, and darkness, which prevent the emergence of the sky's natural color—have dissolved. A very clear openness dawns. Like an autumn sky at dawn, before sunrise, free from any sullying factors, nothing else appears. This deepest consciousness is called the "fundamental innate mind of clear light" and "all-empty" because it is beyond the eighty conceptions and the three subtle minds.

Physically: (1) The white and red drops dissolve into the indestructible drop at the heart—the white dissolving into its white top and the red dissolving into its red bottom. (2) Thereupon, the winds inside the central channel dissolve into the very subtle life-bearing wind. (3) This causes the very subtle wind and the mind of clear light to manifest.

For most people death occurs when the subtlest level of mind manifests. The most subtle consciousness usually remains in the body for three days, unless the body has been ravaged by disease, in which case it might not remain even a day. For a capable practitioner, this is a valuable opportunity for practice. Those who are conscious of the mind of clear light can remain in this state for longer periods and, depending on previous training, can even use it to realize the truth of the emptiness of inherent existence of all phenomena, including cyclic existence and nirvana.

REALIZING EMPTINESS

Understanding the Buddhist doctrine of emptiness is crucial to living and dying with realism and without fear. Emptiness does not mean nonexistence. You might think that emptiness means nothingness, but it does not. What are phenomena empty of? Without understanding what is negated, you cannot understand its absence, or emptiness. Look at it this way: Buddha frequently said that because all phenomena are dependently arisen, they are relative, meaning their existence depends on causes and conditions and on their own parts. Your body, for instance, does not exist independently; rather, it depends on a great many causes such as ovum and sperm as well as food and water. It also depends upon its own parts—legs, arms, torso, and head.

Examine whether your body, appearing as if it exists in its own right, is the same or different from your arms, legs, torso, and head. If it does exist the way it appears, so concretely present, it should become clearer and clearer under the light of analyzing whether the body is any of its individual parts, or whether it is their sum, or whether it is something altogether different. The closer you look, the more it is not found in any of these ways.

This is the case for all phenomena. The fact that you cannot find them under such analysis means that they do not exist under their own power; they are not self-established. They do not inherently exist, despite all appearances to the contrary.

Still, this does not mean that sentient beings and things do not exist at all. Rather, they just do not exist the way they appear to so concretely exist. When you analyze and meditate well, you will understand the harmony between the actual appearance of persons and things and their emptiness of inherent existence. Without such understanding, emptiness and appearance seem to prohibit one another.

All phenomena—causes and effects, agents and actions, good and bad—merely exist conventionally; they are dependent-arisings. Because phenomena depend upon other factors for their existence, they are not independent. This absence of independence—or emptiness of inherent existence—is their ultimate truth. Comprehending this is wisdom.

The fundamental cause of suffering is ignorance—the mistaken conception that living beings and objects inherently exist. All faulty states of mind have this mistake at their root. A principal aim of the spiritual path is to counteract and remove ignorance through wisdom. A wise consciousness, grounded in reality, understands that living beings and other phenomena do not inherently exist. This is the wisdom of emptiness.

One of the most impressive and useful of the First Panchen Lama's writings is his *Argument with Ignorance*, which is similar to the eighth chapter of Shantideva's *Guide to the Bodhisattva's Way of Life*, in which there is an argument between self-centeredness and cherishing others. The First Panchen Lama's *Argument with Ignorance* has a heated discussion between the ignorant misconception that sentient beings and objects exist inherently and the wisdom of dependent-arising and emptiness. When I read that book, I realized that my view of the Middle Way fell short of the highest approach.

Due to his explanation I eventually realized that it is extremely difficult, after refuting inherent existence, to posit the merely nominal and imputed existence of persons and phenomena. This was confirmed by a stanza in Tsongkhapa's great exposition of special insight in his *The Great Treatise on the Stages of the Path to Enlightenment*:

Though for your mind it is difficult to posit the
  dependent-arising

Of cause and effect within the absence of
    inherent existence,
It would be wonderful if you rely on an approach
Saying that such is the system of the Middle Way.

Previously, I was not challenging how sentient beings and objects appear to us. I had left that appearance untouched, and considered the negation of inherent existence as something beyond basic, conventional appearance. Through reflecting on the meaning of the First Panchen Lama's text, however, I developed new understanding. This can best be explained by how I came to view a statement by the late-eighteenth- and early-nineteenth-century Tibetan scholar-yogi Gungtang Könchok Tenpay Drönmay:

Due to the fact that inherent existence is being
    sought under analysis,
Not finding it refutes inherent existence.
Still, not finding it does not negate the basis of
    what is being sought,
And thus afterward a merely nominal remainder
    is seen.

He seems to be indicating that, aside from refuting inherent existence *in addition to* the phenomenon, the appearance of the phenomenon itself is not being refuted. Indeed, the phenomenon itself is not refuted, but it seems that in his statement karmic appearances of phenomena are left untouched in the way that they appear to us to be established by way of their own character, and some additional inherent existence is being refuted. However, this is the perspective of the lower of the two Middle Way Schools, the Autonomy School.

For them, if phenomena were ultimately established, they would be established as their own mode of being, in which case they would have to appear to wisdom of the ultimate, but since phenomena such as the four elements do not appear to wisdom of the ultimate, they do not ultimately exist. That is the perspective of the Autonomy School. It seems to me that from such a perspective, contrary to the statement by Tsongkhapa about the perspective of the higher of the two Middle Way Schools cited above, it would *not* be difficult to posit the dependent-arising of cause and effect in the face of such analysis.

The First Panchen Lama's *Argument with Ignorance* makes clear that when forms and so forth appear to us, right from the start they appear to be established by way of their own character, and thus when this appearance is refuted, it seems as if the phenomenon itself no longer stands. This is why Tsongkhapa says that it is *difficult* to posit the dependent-arising of cause and effect within the absence of inherent existence. Aided by the First Panchen Lama's *Argument with Ignorance,* I understood that what Tsongkhapa said was really so. The book was truly helpful.

Realizing that you do not inherently exist through using the reason that you are neither one nor many, singular nor plural, and maintaining that perspective does undermine—a little—the ignorance conceiving inherent existence. However, this realization does not completely overcome the conception of inherent existence, which remains with respect to yourself. Why? Because a conventional, inherently existent "I" remains for that consciousness. As soon as the "I" appears, along with it the inherent existence that is to be refuted appears, so what you need is the realization that the "I" that appears upon observing mind and body does not exist. *This "I" does not exist.* As the First Panchen Lama says:

Merely refuting the true existence
Of the "I" appearing upon observing mind and
body,

Take this very absence as the object of your
   attention,
With clear appearance without letting its force
   deteriorate.

He is saying that if you meditate this way, it will undermine the conception of inherent existence. This helped me a lot.

Here in the stages of dying you seek to take this ultimate nature of phenomena, the emptiness of inherent existence, as an object of the subtler, more powerful minds and concentrate one-pointedly on it. Through this yoga you will know your own ultimate nature. Of the two natures, conventional and ultimate, you are taking to mind the ultimate—the absence of inherent existence.

SUMMARY ADVICE

1. Notice how various attitudes and conceptions have different strengths in terms of the movement of wind to their respective objects.
2. Learn that after the four internal signs of mirage, smoke, fireflies, and flame (of a butter lamp or of a

candle, at first flickering and then steady), three more subtle minds of vivid white appearance, red-orange increase-of-appearance, and black near-attainment dawn.

3. Remember that you are seeking to use these more subtle minds to realize the truth of emptiness.

4. Emptiness does not mean nonexistence; rather, it is the lack of inherent existence of phenomena, both of beings and things.

5. Learn to analyze phenomena: Focus on whether they are any of their parts individually, or the collection of their parts, or something else entirely. This will show that phenomena do not exist in the concrete way they seem to.

6. All causes and effects, agents and actions, good and bad merely exist conventionally; they are dependent-arisings.

7. Their absence of independence, or emptiness of inherent existence, is their ultimate truth. This is what wisdom understands, undermining the ignorance behind lust and hatred and the suffering they cause.

8. Through this yoga know your own ultimate nature as well as that of all phenomena.

8

The Clear Light of Death

Realize that the body is impermanent like a clay vessel.
Know that phenomena are without inherent
existence, like mirages.
Having destroyed the poisonous weapons of attachment—
attractive like flowers—
You will pass beyond even the sights of death.

—BUDDHA

Stanza Twelve

May the mother and child clear lights meet
When near-attainment dissolves into the all-empty
And all conceptual multiplications cease and an
experience
Like an autumn sky free from polluting conditions
dawns.

According to Highest Yoga Tantra, there is no mind
more subtle than the mind of clear light; it serves as the
basis of all appearances of cyclic existence and nirvana.

This mind of clear light has existed continuously since beginningless cyclic existence. Since it is not temporary, it is called *fundamental mind,* whereas the minds of black near-attainment, red-orange increase-of-appearance, white appearance, and so on are *newly* produced and bound to cease through the power of conditions and thus are called temporary and adventitious. This all-empty, fundamental innate mind of clear light is the innermost mind.

All other minds can be considered coarse, although there are many levels of coarseness and subtlety among them. Relative to the mind of clear light, even the minds of white appearance, red-orange increase-of-appearance, and black near-attainment—which are subtler than ordinary consciousnesses—are coarse. Compared to the fundamental innate mind of clear light, they are temporary, as are ordinary consciousnesses.

From this perspective, the city of erroneous conceptions of subject and object (mentioned earlier in stanza four) can refer to those phenomena that are produced from actions (karma), which themselves arise out of the coarse conceptuality of grosser levels of consciousness. When you are capable of abiding forever in the innate mind of clear light without regressing through the coarser levels, there is no opportunity for the accumulation of karma. However, to remain constantly in the mind of clear light you must remove the obstructions to omniscience, which are the defilements of the erroneous *appearance* of subject and object as if they inherently exist. When you are able to remain in the mind of clear light, conceptual consciousnesses cease. Until then, you are under the sway of a grosser level of consciousness, of temporary conceptuality, and you accumulate karma.

In the final phase of dying, when all coarse consciousnesses dissolve into the all-empty, which is the clear light or fundamental innate mind, the myriad objects of the world as well as concepts such as sameness and difference have been pacified in this subtlest mind. All appearances of environments and beings have withdrawn of their own accord. If you are able to transform the clear light of death into a fully qualified spiritual consciousness, the mind recognizes its own face, its own nature: the entity of the fundamental mind.

For a non-practitioner, coarse appearances also withdraw. This withdrawal of conventional appearances, however, is not due to a perception of reality attained through meditation. In these final four stages of dying, the winds that serve as the mounts of consciousness become increasingly subtle. When, in the last phase, the temporary winds that carry consciousness have all dissolved, the mind (whether one is a practitioner or nonpractitioner) becomes as if undifferentiated, and an immaculate openness dawns.

But as a practitioner, you seek to go beyond this ordinary emptiness, this mere absence of conventional appearances. When the clear light dawns, seek to realize the extraordinary emptiness of inherent existence with the mind of clear light itself. This will not come about through exertion at the time of the clear light itself, but arises from the force of familiarity gained prior to the phases of dissolution, and from the strong mindfulness of emptiness during the dawning of the three minds of white, red, and black appearance. This confirms the importance of continual training.

The cornerstone of my own practice is reflection on the four basic teachings of impermanence, suffering, emptiness, and selflessness. In addition, as a part of eight different daily ritual practices, I meditate on the stages of dying. I imagine the dissolution of the earth element into water, the water element into fire, and so forth. Though I cannot claim any profound experience, there is a little stoppage of breath when the ritual calls for imagining the dissolving of all appearances. I am sure more complete versions manifest if a practitioner visualizes the dissolutions in a more leisurely and thorough way. Since my daily practices of deity yoga all involve visualizing death, I am habituating myself to the process, and thus at the actual time of death these steps will supposedly be familiar. But whether I will succeed or not, I do not know.

Some of my religious friends, including practitioners of a system called the Great Completeness in the Nyingma order of Tibetan Buddhism, have reported deep experiences of dissolution, but still within the realm of similitudes of the actual ones. Some Tibetans, declared to be clinically dead, have remained without undergoing physical decomposition for quite some time. Just last year, the body of a lama from the Sakya order remained fresh without decomposing for more than twenty days. He "died" in Dharmsala but he remained, while still here in Dharmsala, in meditation; then his body was carried to Rajpur in the Dehra Dun area, where it still remained fresh. It was remarkable. I know of about fifteen Tibetans whose bodies similarly stayed without decomposition—some for a few days, some longer, the maximum being three weeks. My own senior tutor, Ling Rinpochay, remained for thirteen days.

In its best form, this state, when transformed into a spiritual experience, is called a meeting of the mother and the child clear lights. The mother clear light naturally appears when dying through the force of karma. The child clear light is generated by having cultivated the spiritual path, achieved by a yogi's exertion in earlier meditation. The meeting of the mother and child clear lights is not actually a meeting of two entities; rather, the mother clear light of death, which dawns due to karma, turns into a spiritual consciousness, the child clear light. This is the meeting of the mother and the child clear lights.

In another interpretation, the child clear light is taken to be emptiness, and the meeting of the two clear lights means not letting the mother clear light be an ordinary mind of death but using it to take as its object the emptiness of inherent existence—the child clear light. Considering the mother clear light as an ordinary mind of death is the more prevalent interpretation, but the meanings are essentially the same.

SUBTLE DROPS AS BASES
OF SUBTLE MINDS

As described above, manifesting the deeper levels of consciousness is intimately bound to the physical processes of the four elements—earth, water, fire, and wind—especially the fourth, since the winds serve as bases of consciousness. Also involved in the process of dying is a drop of subtle matter at the heart, which contains the most subtle consciousness of the ordinary state.

In the Kalachakra Tantra, another Highest Yoga Tantra spoken by Buddha that came to be widely known in India in the tenth century, there is an intriguing presentation of eight drops of subtle matter at strategic places in the body. These are places of defilement to be purified and potential to be utilized. Like the drop at the heart in the *Guhyasamaja Tantra* (which, as mentioned earlier, is the main system being explained in this book), these eight drops are subtle matter the size of a mustard seed and are composed of the basic white and red constituents; they are also supports of subtle consciousnesses. Predispositions formed by virtuous and nonvirtuous actions are infused into these subtle consciousnesses. Deeds of body, speech, and mind deposit latent tendencies in the consciousnesses that reside in these material drops, where they are stored until certain conditions cause them to manifest as pleasure, pain, and the other events of cyclic existence.

There are two sets of four drops each; each pair works together to create different states of consciousness. The first set is located at (1) the forehead (or crown of the head), (2) throat, (3) heart, and (4) navel; the second set is located at (1) the navel, (2) secret place (the base of the spine), (3) center of the sexual organ, and (4) tip of the sexual organ. The drops at the forehead and the navel produce the state of *wakefulness*; the drops at the throat and the base of the spine produce the state of *dreaming*; the drops at the heart and the center of the sexual organ produce the state of *deep sleep*; and the drops at the navel and the tip of the sexual organ produce the state of *sexual bliss*. As you see, the one drop at the navel contains within it two different predispositions: one produces the waking state in its role as the fourth of the upper set of drops, and the other produces the state of sexual bliss in its role as the first of the lower set of drops.

Each drop contains two types of potencies, pure and

impure. When we are awake, the winds of the upper part of the body collect at the forehead, and the winds of the lower part of the body collect at the navel; the pure potencies produce mere appearances of objects and the impure produce appearances of impure objects. During dreaming, the upper winds collect at the throat and the lower winds collect in the secret region, and the pure potencies produce sheer sounds whereas the impure potencies produce confused speech. In deep sleep, the upper winds collect at the heart and the lower winds collect at the center of the sexual organ, and the pure potencies produce nonconceptual clarity and the impure potencies produce obscurity. During strong sexual arousal, the upper winds collect at the navel and the lower winds collect at the tip of the sexual organ, whereby the pure potencies produce bliss and the impure potencies produce emission or sexual secretion (for males and females).

Spiritual training in the Kalachakra tradition is directed toward purifying these four sets of drops. Through cleansing the drops at the forehead and the navel that produce the appearance of impure objects during wakefulness, objects become appearances of empty forms—forms beyond mere matter. As empty forms, these appearances can be utilized on the path to enlightenment. The drops at the throat and the base of the spine have the capacity to produce mistaken speech, but through cleansing them it is possible to uncover "invincible sounds" for use on the spiritual path. The drops at the heart and the middle of the sexual organ have the ability to produce obscurity, but by cleansing them it becomes possible to utilize nonconceptual wisdom on the spiritual path. The drops at the navel and the tip of the sexual organ have the capacity to produce emission, and through cleansing them bliss can be transformed into immutable great bliss without emission and utilized for spiritual purposes. These positive capacities are developed into higher and higher forms, finally turning into the special diamond-like body, speech, mind, and bliss of a Buddha.

In the Kalachakra system all obstructions binding beings to a state of suffering and limitation that prevent them from being altruistically effective are contained in these four drops. It is not the material of the drops themselves that serves as the basis for karmic infusion of the obstructions; rather, the very subtle winds and minds dwelling in these two sets of four drops are infused with karmic potencies, both virtuous and nonvirtuous. The material drops are the supports for these subtle minds and winds, in much the same way as our gross physical body supports our mind.

Two years ago a Tibetan yogi who practiced the Great Completeness style of meditation in the Nyingma tradition achieved a state of the complete disappearance of his gross physical body, which we call "achieving a rainbow body." His name was Achok, and he was from Nyarong. He studied philosophy from time to time at a Geluk monastic university near Lhasa called Sera, and he also received teachings from my junior tutor Trijang Rinpochay, but his main teacher was the Nyingma lama, Dujom Rinpochay. Although he practiced Tantra according to both the old and new schools of Tibetan Buddhism, his main practice was the recitation of *om mani padme hum* and its accompanying meditation.

Until about three years ago, he frequently said he hoped to have the opportunity of meeting the Dalai Lama in this lifetime. Then, one day he called on his followers to perform offerings for the sake of the Dalai Lama's life. After they made offerings, he surprised them by announcing that he would leave. He put on his saffron monastic robe and told them to seal him inside his room for a week. His disciples followed his request and after a week opened the room to find that he had completely disappeared except for his robe. One of his disciples and a fellow practitioner came to Dharmsala, where they related the story to me and gave me a piece of his robe.

Since he usually remained in retreat as a very simple monk with no pretensions, unlike some lamas, he proved that he was a good practitioner and finally this occurred. You can see the connection between cause and effect. There are others about whom miracles are claimed, but without the proper causes.

In Highest Yoga Tantra, the potencies—that in ordinary life produce impure environments and beings by way of the very subtle wind and mind—are purified through practice of the spiritual path, whereby they are transformed into the pure, altruistic mind, speech, and body of a Buddha. Our aim is to manifest the fundamental innate mind of clear light, the most subtle level of consciousness, and to remain within that level of mind without regressing to grosser levels. However, this purified state is not just mental; it involves body, but a body fashioned from wind, the wind that is the mount of the mind of clear light. The ultimate purpose of these manifestations is to assist others in achieving the same freedom from suffering and limitation.

The center of this process of purification is realization of the luminous and knowing nature of mind—understanding that afflictive emotions such as lust, hatred, enmity, jealousy, and belligerence do not reside in the very essence of mind but are peripheral to it. When the mind knows its own nature and when this knowledge is teamed with powerful concentration, it gradually becomes possible to reduce and finally to overcome the afflictive states that drive the process of repeated suffering. This is the Tibetan view of the intimate relationship between mind and matter, and how they work in the process of altruistically directed purification.

SUMMARY ADVICE

1. The final phase in the process of dying occurs when the fundamental innate mind of clear light dawns. This mind has existed continuously since beginningless time and will continue to exist forever.
2. Eventually, at Buddhahood, you become capable of remaining in the innate mind of clear light without passing through the reverse process of the coarser

levels of consciousness. At that point, there is no opportunity for the accumulation of karma.

3. Even for an ordinary non-practitioner, an absence of coarse appearances dawns at death, but a highly developed practitioner seeks to make use of this mind to realize the truth, the emptiness of inherent existence, through the force of familiarity gained from meditation on emptiness.

4. The ordinary mind of clear light that manifests in the final stage of death is called the mother clear light, and the clear light generated through the force of cultivating the spiritual path is called the child clear light.

5. When the mother clear light of death, which dawns due to karma, turns into a spiritual consciousness knowing emptiness—the child clear light—this transformation is called the meeting of the mother and the child clear lights.

Stanza Thirteen

May we be set in one-pointed profound meditation
In the exalted wisdom of joined innate bliss and
emptiness

*During the four empties upon the melting of the moon-
    like white constituent
By the fire of the lightning-like Powerful Female.*

Through concentration techniques yogis generate
inner heat, called the Powerful Female (*Tumo,* in
Tibetan), which moves upward in the central channel
from its main location in the solar plexus. This inner
heat melts the white constituent in the complex of
channels at the top of the head (the wheel of great
bliss). Metaphorically, this essential white constituent is compared to the moon and called the
mind of enlightenment. As the white constituent
melts, it descends inside the central channel; as it
gradually reaches the channel-wheels of the throat,
heart, navel, and secret region, four levels of joy are
experienced—joy, supreme joy, special joy, and innate
joy.

These four joys are exalted wisdoms of great bliss.
These joyous wisdoms take emptiness as their object of
realization, thus bliss and emptiness are said to be
joined. Through the meditative wisdom of great bliss in
Highest Yoga Tantra, when the mother clear light dawns
at death due to karma, it is possible to transform it into

a spiritual path consciousness (the child clear light). The wish in this stanza of the Panchen Lama's poem—the last concerned with the death state—is directed toward having this capacity.

Someone who practices Highest Yoga Tantra daily imagines the appearance of the eight signs of death—mirage, smoke, fireflies, flame of a butter lamp, vivid white appearance, vivid red-orange increase-of-appearance, vivid black near-attainment, and clear light—in conjunction with reflection on emptiness. This is done within a threefold mindfulness: You identify the sign that is presently appearing, then identify the previous sign, and then identify the next sign. For instance, "Fireflies are appearing. Smoke just passed. A flame is about to appear." Although the eight signs do not actually appear in meditation except for advanced yogis, you maintain the three mindfulnesses in your imagination for the sake of developing familiarity with these signs. In full-fledged practice, when you reach the level of actual cultivation, you remain in meditative concentration on emptiness and the signs appear of their own accord.

DEITY YOGA

In Tantra practice, imagination is used to accelerate spiritual development. Deity yoga requires you (1) to imagine that your mind (even though ordinarily bothered by afflictive emotions) is a mind of pure wisdom motivated by compassion; (2) to substitute the appearance of your ordinary body (composed of flesh, blood, and bone) with a body risen out of compassionately motivated wisdom; and (3) to develop a sense of a pure self based on a purely appearing mind and body in an ideal environment, fully involved in helping others. In these ways you visualize yourself as having a Buddha's body, activities, resources, and surroundings. Imagination is the key. In meditating on yourself in this ideal condition, you begin with reflection on emptiness, developing as much awareness of the emptiness of inherent existence as you can. It is from that awareness that the deity appears. The mind, realizing emptiness, appears as the deity and his or her surroundings, resources, and acts of compassion. In this way, deity yoga is the union of wisdom and compassionate motivation; one consciousness realizes emptiness and also appears in the form of a compassionately active deity.

In the particular practice of deity yoga found in Highest Yoga Tantra, performed six times daily, practitioners similarly first reflect on emptiness, but then they conjoin whatever level of understanding of emptiness they have with the gradual unfolding of the eight signs of death. As a final step, they use the mind of clear light realizing emptiness—or a consciousness mimicking such a state of mind—as the basis out of which they appear in ideal, compassionate form as a deity.

SEXUAL UNION
AND THE SPIRITUAL PATH

A practitioner who has firm compassion and wisdom can make use of sexual intercourse in the spiritual path as a technique for strongly focusing consciousness and manifesting the fundamental innate mind of clear light. Its purpose is to actualize and prolong the deeper levels of mind in order to put their power to use in strengthening the realization of emptiness. Mere intercourse has nothing to do with spiritual cultivation, but when a person has achieved a high level of practice in motivation and wisdom, even the joining of the two sex organs, or

so-called intercourse, does not detract from the main-
tenance of pure behavior.

How does sexual intercourse help in the path? Since
the potential of grosser levels of mind is very limited,
but the deeper, more subtle levels are much more
powerful, developed practitioners need to access these
subtler levels of mind. To do so, grosser consciousness
needs to be weakened and temporarily stopped, and to
accomplish this it is necessary to bring about dramatic
changes in the flow of inner energies. Even though brief
versions of the deeper levels of mind occur during
sneezing and yawning, they obviously cannot be pro-
longed. Also, previous experience with manifesting the
deeper levels is required to make use of their occurrence
in deep sleep. Due to this, sex is utilized. Through special techniques of concentration during orgasm competent practitioners can prolong very deep, subtle, and
powerful states and put them to use to realize emptiness. However, if you engage in sexual intercourse
within an ordinary mental context, there is no benefit.

The father of the late Serkong Rinpochay was both a
great scholar and an accomplished practitioner. He was
from Ganden Monastery a good distance to the southeast
of Lhasa, but his main lama, Trin Ngawang Norbu, was in

Drepung Monastery west of Lhasa. So, Serkong Rinpochay's father used to stay in Lhasa and every day early in the morning made the long trek to Drepung, where he would fetch water for his lama, sweep his place, occasionally receive teachings during the day, and then return to Lhasa.

One night, Serkong's father met a girl and lost his vows. Regretting this very much, the next morning he tearfully went to Drepung, but when he reached the lama's room, the lama had already performed a ceremony of recompense. The teacher, Trin Ngawang Norbu, said, "You have relapsed, but that is right. Now you should practice Tantra with a consort." That in itself was unusual, but, even more extraordinary was that after the consort's death the mantra of the goddess Vajrayogini was manifest right in her skull bone.

There was another lama during the same period, Tabung Rinpochay, who practiced with a consort. One auspicious day of the month, when the Regent and some other senior lamas such as Trijang Rinpochay (who became my junior tutor) were receiving teaching from him, there was a ritual performance that involved two flutelike instruments. The two players used their left and right hands in opposite ways to cover the stops, and thus when they looked back and forth at each other, they ended up playing very different tunes. The entire audience stopped chanting and was raucously laughing at this strange tune. When they looked at Tabung Rinpochay, however, he was sitting there totally unaware of what was happening, but not sleeping. Later, the Regent realized that at that very moment Tabung Rinpochay was receiving teaching from within the plane of pure appearance.

During this period the Thirteenth Dalai Lama conducted an investigation into which lamas were authentic and expelled quite a number of them, but he made an exception for these two, Serkong Rinpochay's father and Tabung Rinpochay. In this way he officially recognized their extraordinary ability and special right to use a consort in the practice of Tantra. Thus they must have had some deeper experiences, but I do not know of any record of their claiming to have done so.

SUMMARY ADVICE

1. The highest level of practitioner can transform the mother clear light, which dawns at death due to karma, into a spiritual path consciousness.

2. On lower levels, those who daily practice the deity yoga of Highest Yoga Tantra imagine the appearance of the eight signs of death within a threefold mindfulness, identifying the sign that is appearing, the previous sign, and the one coming up. Practice the series of eight in conjunction with reflection on emptiness. Each has three parts, except for the first and last, which have two:

- ◆ Mirage is appearing. Smoke is about to dawn.
- ◆ Smoke is appearing. Mirage just passed. Fireflies are about to dawn.
- ◆ Fireflies are appearing. Smoke just passed. A flame is about to dawn.
- ◆ A flame is appearing. Fireflies just passed. A vivid white appearance is about to dawn.
- ◆ A vivid white appearance is appearing. A flame just passed. A vivid red-orange increase is about to dawn.
- ◆ A vivid red-orange increase is appearing. A vivid white appearance just passed. A vivid blackness is about to dawn.
- ◆ A vivid blackness is appearing. A vivid red-

orange increase just passed. The mind of clear light is about to dawn.

◆ The mind of clear light is appearing. A vivid blackness just passed.

3. In the particular practice of deity yoga in Highest Yoga Tantra, practitioners conjoin whatever level of understanding of emptiness they have with the gradual unfolding of the eight signs of death. Then they use the mind of clear light realizing emptiness—or a consciousness mimicking such a state of mind—as the basis out of which they appear in ideal, compassionate form as a deity.

4. Highly developed practitioners who have firm compassion and wisdom can make use of sexual intercourse as a technique to strongly focus the mind and manifest the fundamental innate mind of clear light. With this innermost mind they realize the emptiness of inherent existence in a dramatically powerful way.

Reacting to the Intermediate State

Those who decide "I will die" stop being afraid.
How could they fear even the visions of death!

—BUDDHA

Stanza Fourteen

May we complete in place of the intermediate state
The concentrated meditation of illusion so that upon
*   leaving the clear light*
We rise in a Body of Complete Enjoyment blazing with
*   the glory of a Buddha's marks and beauties*
Arisen from the mere wind and mind of the clear light
*   of death.*

When yogis rise from the realization of emptiness by
the most subtle mind, they do so in a body fashioned
out of mere wind (energy) and mind, adorned with the

marks and beauties of a Buddha. This is not just imagination or imitation, but fact. Instead of entering into an intermediate state, the yogi rises from the death state in what we call an illusory body, in place of the intermediate state. It can be of two different types—either an impure illusory body or a Buddha's Complete Enjoyment Body. This stanza is a wish to accomplish such a profound transformation.

The mind of clear light and the wind that serves as the mount of the clear light are one entity, but they can be divided conceptually. The wind serves as the substantial cause of an illusory body, whereas the mind serves as the cooperative condition of an illusory body. These two causes produce an illusory body similar in aspect to the body of the favorite deity that you have been imagining through the practice of deity yoga. It is not a body of flesh and bone. It has a nature simply of wind and mind, clear and unhindered like a rainbow.

The appearance of the ideal being, the deity, is said to be like the sudden appearance of a fish leaping out of a lake in full form. For a long time you have been meditating on yourself as a particular deity, cultivating that vision, imagining this ideal body in preparation for this transformation. The goal of this practice has finally been realized. Imitation has led to fact.

LEVELS OF PRACTICE

All along I have tried to emphasize the importance of practicing at your natural level. Within Highest Yoga Tantra there are three levels. To this point, we have been considering practitioners who have achieved a high level of proficiency but have not been able to achieve the supreme feat of Buddhahood in this lifetime. Such people begin to die due to the force of polluted karma and afflictive emotions, but if they are able to transform the mother clear light of death into the child clear light of the path, they can bypass an ordinary intermediate state leading to rebirth, and achieve an *actual* illusory body, not one that is just imagined.

The next level of practitioner (discussed in the following stanza) is not able to transform the clear light of death into a spiritual path state—and therefore cannot induce achievement of an illusory body—but still does not undergo ordinary death. This yogi does transform the clear light of death into a *form* of the path, albeit one that is not capable of producing an illusory body. The yogi is able to appear, not in fact but in imagination, in an illusory body during an ordinary intermediate state. A yogi at this level can choose the form of rebirth through the power of compassion, wishes, and mindfulness.

The next level of practitioner (discussed in stanza sixteen) cannot transform the clear light of death into any fully qualified path but is able, after the period of unconsciousness in the latter part of the mind of black near-attainment, to generate mindfulness of Tantra practice in some form during the manifestation of the clear light. This person passes into an ordinary intermediate state and takes rebirth in an ordinary way, but is capable of generating beneficial practice through good predispositions—the projective force of former actions—and the coming together of external and internal circumstances.

All three levels are seeking to generate the clear light consciousness into a wisdom realizing emptiness. Therefore, prior to the stages of dissolution, all three levels become mindful of emptiness. Especially during the dissolutions of earth, water, fire, and wind and the emergence of the four empties—the minds of white appearance, red-orange increase-of-appearance, black near-attainment, and clear light—they generate the power of mindfulness and contemplate the emptiness of inherent existence, the deathless mode of being that is the nature of all phenomena.

Since the top level of practitioner is capable of transforming the clear light of death into a consciousness realizing emptiness, this acts as an antidote to powerless death. From that time on, you are no longer susceptible to birth and death. The true nature of all phenomena, contemplated in this way, yields immortality (consequently, it is called "deathless" in the poem).

Death dawns in stages, from the dissolving of earth into water, through to and including the dawning of the clear light. Afterward, in cases of ordinary death (not the death of the most highly trained yogi) the eight stages occur in reverse order: passing from the clear light to black near-attainment, to red-orange increase-of-appearance, to white appearance, to flame, to fireflies, to smoke, to mirage. At the end of an ordinary death, three events occur simultaneously: (1) the clear light ceases; (2) you rise from the clear light of death into the vivid black near-attainment; and (3) the intermediate state begins (after which the other reverse steps occur). In a similar way, a yogi—on the first level of Highest Yoga Tantra practice but dwelling in the metaphoric clear light—simultaneously rises from the clear light into near-attainment, creating an illusory body. However, a yogi on the first level of Highest Yoga Tantra practice who rises from the *actual* clear light does not pass backward to the mind of near-attainment and so forth; all coarser levels of mind have ceased.

SUMMARY ADVICE

1. Highly developed practitioners are able to utilize the common clear light of death and the wind on which it rides as the substantial causes of pure mind and body, respectively.

2. To be able to rise from within the mind of clear light in a pure body fashioned from wind, it is necessary to have previously practiced imagining yourself as having altruistically motivated mind and body. What is performed in imitation eventually leads to what is accomplished in fact.

3. Bringing about the final transformation requires not passing backward from the fundamental innate mind

of clear light to a coarser level of mind. This yields a deathless state.

Stanza Fifteen

If, due to karma, an intermediate state is established,
May erroneous appearances be purified
Through immediately analyzing and realizing the
    absence of inherent existence
Of the sufferings of birth, death, and intermediate state.

At the end of the period during which the subtlest mind remains in the body, there is a slight movement of the wind on which the mind of clear light rides, and the most subtle wind and most subtle consciousness leave the opened drop of white and red constituents at the heart and exit the body. A small amount of blood emerges from the nose and a small amount of essential white fluid emerges from the sexual organ, indicating that this final level of consciousness has left the body, although these signs might not occur in those whose bodies have been wasted by disease. At this point the body begins to rot and smell.

The best of those yogis who do not achieve Buddhahood during their lifetime achieve an illusory body in place of an intermediate state. Ordinary people unable to rise in an illusory body because they have not attained the higher realizations pass into an ordinary intermediate state through the force of karma. If this happens, you should immediately recognize and understand your situation.

When the clear light ceases and the remaining seven states start to dawn in reverse order, this marks the beginning of the intermediate state. Here, at the opening of the state between lives, you pass through the eight phases just as you do when waking up, beginning a dream, coming to from fainting, and emerging from orgasm:

8. clear light
7. vivid black mind-sky
6. vivid red-orange mind-sky
5. vivid white mind-sky
4. flame of a lamp
3. fireflies
2. smoke
1. mirage

Just as when you go to sleep you reemerge with a dream-body, so in the intermediate state you suddenly have a body shaped like that in which you will be reborn.

This body is often like your future body at around age five or six. Like a dream-body, it is made from a wind-mind combination. The wind on which the mind of clear light rides is the substantial cause of that body, but it also is a cooperative condition contributing to the mind of the intermediate state. The mind of clear light, conversely, is the substantial cause of the mind of the intermediate state and the cooperative condition contributing to the body of the intermediate state being.

There was a monk-official from the Geluk order, a good practitioner and also courageous. When the Chinese Liberation Army came to Chamdo in the Kham Province of Tibet and "liberated" it, he was a subordinate to the representative of the Tibetan government near that area. The representative felt that it was important to meet with the Chinese and asked his subordinates if there was anyone willing to meet them, but everyone except this monk-official and another was afraid to go. This trusted and courageous man related to me that on one occasion his mother told him, "I will go into deep sleep and don't touch my body." For a week she was in deep sleep, after which she returned. During that week her soul, or mind, visited various places. Her son had no reason to lie to me, and he was not just reporting a rumor. This was not a case of dying and returning from death but most likely a special dream-body.

In the intermediate state, because your body is fashioned from wind and mind, you have all five senses, but your body is clear like a rainbow, casting no shadow, and you do not leave footprints. By the magical force of karma you are naturally endowed with the ability to travel in a very short time around or through this world system unimpeded by earth, rock, mountains, and buildings; nevertheless, once you have entered your new mother's womb, you cannot leave. Although you speak to your relatives, friends, and others, they do not hear you and thus do not answer in return. You do not see sun, moon, or stars. Despite your not having had clairvoyance previously, you have limited clairvoyance now.

If you find that you show signs of being in this state, you should think, "I have died and I am now dwelling in the intermediate state." Use the power of mindfulness to realize that pleasant and unpleasant appearances during the intermediate state are the creations of a mistaken mind, and use mindfulness to understand that there is no point in being attached to the pleasant, or angered by the unpleasant. Instead, imagine that you have risen in an illusory body, realizing that the various appearances and sufferings of death, intermediate state, and rebirth are without inherent existence, that they are not true. Know that these appearances are due to former actions (karma), which do not, in fact, have even a particle of true establishment.

Just as in deity yoga you actively imagine that everything is limitlessly pure, fashioned from compassion and wisdom, so here in the intermediate state you view all appearances of beings as gods and goddesses and all appearances of environments as wondrous mansions, thereby detaching yourself from any dislike for the ugly or attraction to the beautiful. You are seeking to cause whatever appears to dawn as empty of inherent existence, and whatever is empty to emerge as the sport of bliss, the sport of a deity.

SUMMARY ADVICE

1. It is very important to recognize the signs that you are in the intermediate state.
2. View all pleasant and unpleasant appearances and experiences as expressions of your own good and bad karma.

3. In place of what is presented to you, imagine that you have risen in an illusory body, imagining all appearances of beings as ideal expressions of compassion and wisdom and all appearances of environments as wondrous mansions.

4. Refrain from disliking the ugly or liking the beautiful.

5. Realize that the various appearances and sufferings of death, intermediate state, and rebirth are empty of inherent existence; they do not exist in their own right.

Stanza Sixteen

May we be born in a pure land
Through yoga transforming the external, internal,
    and secret
When various signs—four sounds of the reversal
    of the elements,
Three frightful appearances, and uncertainties—
    appear.

While you are alive, all winds and conceptions are sunk in ordinary patterns and not under your control.

During the intermediate state, the winds, or energies, associated with the four elements reverse their usual patterns, and frightful sounds emerge from this reversal. When the earth-wind collapses, a sound like mountains crumbling loudly rumbles. When the water-wind collapses, a sound like an ocean in uproar crashes. When the fire-wind collapses, a sound like fire blazing in a heavy forest rages. Due to the collapse of the wind-wind, a sound like a horrendous whirling hurricane howls. There are also frightful appearances of hell-beings, hungry ghosts, and animals that are projections of your own karma. Some appear as Lords of Death, brandishing their weapons and shouting, "Strike! Kill," and you are frightened.

Your place, reliance, behavior, food, friends, and feelings are completely uncertain. Uncertainty of place means that you constantly arrive in various places. Uncertainty of reliance means that you seek refuge in the transient: bridges, wells, and so forth. Uncertainty of behavior means that you abruptly change and waft about like a feather on the wind. Uncertainty of food means that you see delicious foods but are unable to eat them unless they have been intended for you. Uncertainty of friends means that you take up company with random beings. Uncertainty of feeling means that you experience sudden changes in mood—sometimes happy, sometimes pained, sometimes sad, angry, and so forth.

In addition, in the intermediate state there are the three frightful ravines that appear—a great red ravine if you are dominated by lust, a great gray ravine if you are dominated by ignorance, and a great black ravine if you are dominated by hatred. There are also four paths indicating your next life. If wherever you go there is a path of white light, it is a sign that you will be born as a god or demigod. If the path is yellow light, your next life will be as a human or an animal. If it is a path of black light, it indicates rebirth as a hell-being. If it is a path of red light, it suggests rebirth as a hungry ghost.

In the intermediate state, the color of the body of someone to be reborn as a hell-being is like a burnt log; as an animal, like smoke; as a hungry ghost, like water; as a god of the desire realm or as a human, like gold; as a god of the form realm, white. The direction of your movement, too, reflects your rebirth. The intermediate forms of hell-beings, hungry ghosts, and animals proceed downward headfirst. The intermediate forms of gods of the realm of desire (states of rebirth characterized by high enjoyment) and humans go straight forward. The intermediate states of gods of the form realm (states of rebirth characterized by intense concentration) go upward.

The intermediate state could be as short as an instant, especially if your virtuous karma is particularly strong, as would be the case if you had generated powerful love and compassion, or developed a powerful wish to be reborn in a Pure Land, or when your intention to be reborn for the benefit of others is powerful. The intermediate state could also be as short as an instant if your nonvirtuous karma is particularly strong, from, for example, killing a parent. Otherwise, driven by karma in varying degrees of darkness and light, you will rush about seeking a situation for rebirth. If it is not found within seven days, the intermediate being dies. Just as when you begin to awaken from sleep your dream-body dissolves like breath on a mirror, your wind-body in the intermediate state dissolves from the bottom and the top, ending at the heart. In this small death, you quickly pass through the eight phases of death in forward order, but you re-emerge into a new intermediate state—again through the reverse order. At the most, this seven-day process can continue through seven such "rebirths" in the intermediate state, making forty-nine days. Some say that a day here is relative to the length of a day for the type of being as which you will be reborn—this being extremely long for some beings—but others say it is the length of a human day.

Returning to the poem: In the midst of these various appearances, you are seeking to remain calm and to cause (1) your external environments to appear as wondrous inestimable mansions and their surroundings, (2) internal beings (such as hell-beings, hungry ghosts, animals, humans, demigods, and gods) to appear as deities (beings whose very essence is compassion and wisdom), and (3) the secret (your own awareness and thoughts) to appear as the concentrated meditation of bliss realizing emptiness. Thus, no matter what signs appear, they are reversible by practice, through which there is no doubt that you will be reborn in a good life. Through the power of the three yogas imagining the external, internal, and secret to be pure, you are seeking to close the door of rebirth to an impure life in cyclic existence and, instead, be reborn in a special, supreme land beyond polluted karma and afflictive emotions where you can continue practice.

SUMMARY ADVICE

1. Be prepared that in the intermediate state there may be many unusual appearances, both wonderful and horrific. Understand now that whatever appears can be transformed by your imagination.
2. Be calm. Imagine the environment as beautiful mansions laid out in a serene landscape. See beings as having an essence of compassion and wisdom. Consider your own awareness as a blissful mind realizing emptiness.
3. This will yield rebirth in a place where you can continue your practice toward deeper spiritual realization.

10

Taking a Positive Rebirth

No matter what fortune you have gained,
When you depart for another life
You are alone without spouse or children,
Without clothing, without friends,
Like someone conquered by a foe in the desert.
If you will not have even your own name,
What need to consider anything else?

—BUDDHA

Stanza Seventeen

May we be reborn with the supreme life support of a
  Tantra practitioner using the sky
Or the body of a monastic or lay practitioner possessing
  the three practices
And may we complete the realizations of the paths of the
  two stages of generation and completion,
Thereby attaining quickly a Buddha's Bodies—Truth,
  Complete Enjoyment, and Emanation.

Connecting to the next life while in the intermediate state is a process of attraction and repulsion. Both animals that are born from eggs outside the body and beings born from wombs either see their parents actually in the process of sex, or an image of this, and then generate desire for the parent of the opposite sex and repulsion toward the parent of the same sex. When the intermediate being is about to embrace the one it desires, suddenly all it sees is that person's sexual organ, and so it gets angry. In this way, attraction and repulsion bring about the final death of the intermediate-state being.

We have to say that this is the way that the intermediate state *sometimes* ends, since in vitro fertilization contradicts what some of our texts say has to be the case—specifically, that the parents have to be lying together under a condition of strong sexual arousal. Nowadays, the father's semen may be kept in a laboratory and inserted into the mother's womb without any sexual arousal. This procedure contradicting certain scriptures is now a reality, and we must accept it. As followers of the tradition of Nalanda Monastic University in ancient India, we must accept reason and investigation. From that viewpoint our usual explanation is incomplete.

Even in Buddhist scriptures there is a story of a married couple who became celibate—one a monk and the other a nun. One day the male, influenced by memories of his past, chased his former wife. On touching her body, his semen was emitted onto her clothing. Later, she also came under the influence of her memories and put some of his ejaculate inside her vagina. In time, a child was born. So, even this early Buddhist scripture contradicts the doctrine that conception only takes place while the couple is in sexual embrace.

In a similar way, it is said that Shakyamuni Buddha's own lineage is traced back to an individual whose name was Sun-Friend because his father's seminal fluid, which had fallen on a leaf, was enhanced by the warmth of the sun such that two children formed. These two stories, that once seemed to be fairy tales, are now being realized in science. Although generally it is the case that conception occurs under certain conditions, it is not always so. Similarly, the end of the intermediate state does not *necessarily* require attraction to the parent of the opposite sex and frustration at finally seeing only the sexual organ.

During the death of the intermediate state, the being quickly passes through the eight phases in forward order:

1. mirage
2. smoke
3. fireflies
4. flame of a lamp
5. vivid white mind-sky
6. vivid red-orange mind-sky
7. vivid black mind-sky
8. clear light

At the moment of conception, the being passes through the remaining seven in reverse order:

7. vivid black mind-sky
6. vivid red-orange mind-sky
5. vivid white mind-sky
4. flame of a lamp
3. fireflies
2. smoke
1. mirage

There are differing explanations for how the being enters the womb. Some texts say it is by entering into the male's mouth or top of the head and passing through his body and phallus into the female's womb. Other texts say that the being enters directly through the female's vagina into the womb. A person with virtue predominating will have a sense of entering into a pleasant house and hearing pleasant sounds. A person dominated by non-virtue will have a sense of entering into a swamp or dark forest in the midst of raucous clamor.

The very subtle wind and mind of the being enters the material (egg and sperm) contributed by the parents. In the fetus, which at this time is the size of a large mustard seed, the central channel forms with the right and left channels circling it three times. Then the upward-moving wind and downward-voiding wind move in their respective directions and the three channels become extended. The body gradually develops and eventually emerges from the womb.

By continually sustaining the spiritual practice explained in the preceding stanzas of the First Panchen Lama's poem, you can be reborn with a special physical body supporting a life in which you will be capable of finishing the remaining Tantra paths that lead to full enlightenment. You can be reborn in unusual places inhabited by beings called "sky-users," who are practicing Tantra, or in other, more ordinary places where teaching, gurus, and freedom to practice exist. In such a favorable rebirth you would take vows of pure behavior and come to possess the three practices—morality, concentrated meditation, and wisdom—as the root of your spiritual advancement. With these as your foundation, you would seek to complete the realizations of the two stages of Highest Yoga Tantra:

- ◆ deity yoga coupled with meditation on emptiness and the eight signs of death
- ◆ deity yoga with meditation on emptiness, withdrawal of the winds in the central channel, and actualization of the more profound levels of consciousness

Through these stages, you would complete the remaining steps to Buddhahood, a state of full service to others. The final wish in the Panchen Lama's poem is for just such a future life. Remember, the ultimate goal of Buddhist practice is to serve others, and for the most effective state of service it is necessary to achieve pure mind and body. The aim is to be able to help a vast number of sentient beings through myriad means.

When you practice, do not let the path just be something outside of yourself, but turn your own mind into the spiritual path. Otherwise, though you try to practice, you may become tired and even annoyed after a while. Do not just recite the words of the First Panchen Lama's poem, *Wishes for Release from the Perilous Straits of the Intermediate State, Hero Releasing from Fright,* but practice it daily from the approach of reflective meditation, taking the meaning to the mind. That is my advice.

SUMMARY ADVICE

1. Aim in your rebirth to be reborn with a body and in a situation capable of finishing the remaining spiritual paths.
2. The purpose of becoming fully enlightened is to fully serve others.

II

Daily Reflection on the Poem

Just as the strong current of a waterfall
Cannot be reversed,
So the movement of a human life
Is also irreversible.

—BUDDHA

Here is the First Panchen Lama's poem in its entirety.

*Wishes for Release from the Perilous Straits of the
Intermediate State, Hero Releasing from Fright*
By the First Panchen Lama,
Losang Chokyi Gyeltsen

1.

*I and all beings throughout space and without exception
Go for refuge until the ultimate of enlightenments
To the past, present, and future Buddhas, the Doctrine,
and the Spiritual Community.*

May we be released from the frights of this life, the
　　intermediate state, and the next.

2.

May we extract the meaningful essence of this life
　　support
Without being distracted by the senseless affairs of this
　　life,
Since this good foundation, hard to gain and easy to
　　disintegrate,
Presents an opportunity of choice between profit and
　　loss, comfort and misery.

3.

May we realize that there is no time to waste,
Death being definite but the time of death indefinite.
What has gathered will separate, what has been
　　accumulated will be consumed without residue,
At the end of a rising comes descent, the finality of
　　birth is death.

4.

May we be relieved from overwhelming suffering due to
　　the various causes of death

When in this city of erroneous conceptions of subject
    and object
The illusory body composed of the four impure elements
And consciousness are about to separate.

5.

May we be relieved from mistaken appearances of non-
    virtue
When, deceived at the time of need by this body
    sustained so dearly,
The frightful enemies—the lords of death—manifest
And we kill ourselves with the weapons of the three
    poisons of lust, hatred, and bewilderment.

6.

May we remember instructions for practice
When doctors forsake us and rites are of no avail,
Friends have given up hope for our life,
And we are left with nothing else to do.

7.

May we have the confidence of joy and delight
When food and wealth accumulated with miserliness
    are left behind

And we separate forever from cherished and longed-for
friends,
Going alone to a perilous situation.

8.

May we generate a powerful mind of virtue
When the elements—earth, water, fire, and wind—
dissolve in stages
And physical strength is lost, mouth and nose dry and
pucker,
Warmth withdraws, breaths are gasped, and rattling
sounds emerge.

9.

May we realize the deathless mode of being
When various mistaken appearances frightful and
horrible
And in particular mirage, smoke, and fireflies appear
And the mounts of the eighty indicative conceptions cease.

10.

May we generate strong mindfulness and introspection
When the wind constituent begins to dissolve into
consciousness

And the external continuum of breath ceases, coarse
    dualistic appearances dissolve,
And an appearance like a burning butter lamp dawns.

11.

May we know our own nature ourselves
Through the yoga realizing cyclic existence and nirvana
    as empty
When appearance, increase, and near-attainment
    dissolve—the earlier into the later—
And experiences like pervasive moonlight, sunlight, and
    darkness dawn.

12.

May the mother and child clear lights meet
When near-attainment dissolves into the all-empty
And all conceptual multiplications cease and an
    experience
Like an autumn sky free from polluting conditions dawns.

13.

May we be set in one-pointed profound meditation
In the exalted wisdom of joined innate bliss and
    emptiness

During the four empties upon the melting of the moon-
    like white constituent
By the fire of the lightning-like Powerful Female.

14.

May we complete in place of the intermediate state
The concentrated meditation of illusion so that upon
    leaving the clear light
We rise in a Body of Complete Enjoyment blazing with
    the glory of a Buddha's marks and beauties
Arisen from the mere wind and mind of the clear light of
    death.

15.

If, due to karma, an intermediate state is established,
May erroneous appearances be purified
Through immediately analyzing and realizing the
    absence of inherent existence
Of the sufferings of birth, death, and intermediate state.

16.

May we be born in a pure land
Through yoga transforming the external, internal, and
    secret

When various signs—four sounds of the reversal of the
    elements,
Three frightful appearances, and uncertainties—
    appear.

17.

May we be reborn with the supreme life support of a
    Tantra practitioner using the sky
Or the body of a monastic or lay practitioner possessing
    the three practices
And may we complete the realizations of the paths of the
    two stages of generation and completion,
Thereby attaining quickly a Buddha's Bodies—Truth,
    Complete Enjoyment, and Emanation.

APPENDIX:

Outline of the Poem and Summary Advice

Here is an outline of the poem, together with the summary advice for each stanza.

*Wishes for Release from the Perilous Straits of the
Intermediate State, Hero Releasing from Fright*
By the First Panchen Lama,
Losang Chokyi Gyeltsen

STANZA ONE: WITHIN REFUGE AND CARING FOR OTHERS,
WISHING FOR PROTECTION FROM THE FRIGHTS OF THIS
LIFE, THE INTERMEDIATE STATE, AND THE NEXT (P. 73)

*I and all beings throughout space and without exception
Go for refuge until the ultimate of enlightenments*

> *To the past, present, and future Buddhas, the Doctrine,*
> *and the Spiritual Community.*
> *May we be released from the frights of this life, the*
> *intermediate state, and the next.*

1. The motivation for your practice should be the benefit of all living beings—their freedom from suffering and attainment of perfection. Always adjust your motivation toward helping others as much as possible. At least try to do no harm.

2. Buddhas are teachers of the spiritual path; they do not give realization like a gift. You have to practice morality, concentrated meditation, and wisdom on a daily basis.

STANZA TWO: WITHIN CONTEMPLATING THE
MEANINGFULNESS AND DIFFICULTY OF FINDING
THIS LIFE SUPPORT, WISHING TO EXTRACT ITS
ESSENCE (P. 79)

> *May we extract the meaningful essence of this life*
> *support*
> *Without being distracted by the senseless affairs of*
> *this life,*

*Since this good foundation, hard to gain and easy to
  disintegrate,
Presents an opportunity of choice between profit and
  loss, comfort and misery.*

1. Realize the value of the human body with which you
   have been endowed, for it is the result of many past
   good causes. Appreciate the fact that teachings are
   available and ready to be implemented.

2. Since this precious human life can be used in powerfully beneficial or destructive ways, and is itself most
   fragile, make good use of it now.

3. Physical happiness is just an occasional balance of
   elements in the body, not a deep harmony. Understand the temporary for what it is.

4. A tamed mind makes you peaceful, relaxed, and
   happy, whereas if your mind is not peaceful and
   tamed, no matter how wonderful your external
   circumstances, you will be beset by frights
   and worries. Realize that the root of your own
   happiness and welfare rests with a peaceful and
   tamed mind. It is also a great benefit to those
   around you.

STANZA THREE: WITHIN MINDFULNESS OF
IMPERMANENCE AND DEATH, WISHING TO OVERCOME
ATTACHMENT TO CYCLIC EXISTENCE (P. 89)

> *May we realize that there is no time to waste,*
> *Death being definite but the time of death indefinite.*
> *What has gathered will separate, what has been*
> *   accumulated will be consumed without residue,*
> *At the end of a rising comes descent, the finality of birth*
> *   is death.*

1. If you cultivate a sense of the uncertainty of the time of death, you will make better use of your time.

2. To prevent procrastination with regard to spiritual practice, take care not to come under the influence of the illusion of permanence.

3. Realize that no matter how wonderful a situation may be, its nature is such that it must end.

4. Do not think that there will be time later.

5. Be frank about facing your own death. Skillfully encourage others to be frank about their deaths. Do not deceive each other with compliments when the time of death is near. Honesty will foster courage and joy.

STANZA FOUR: WISHING FOR THE NONARISING OF
OVERWHELMING SUFFERING WHILE DYING (P. 99)

> *May we be relieved from overwhelming suffering due to*
>   *the various causes of death*
> *When in this city of erroneous conceptions of subject*
>   *and object*
> *The illusory body composed of the four impure elements*
> *And consciousness are about to separate.*

1. Practice now so that at the time of death the force
   of your familiarity with virtue will affect your attitude.

2. View the body as a veritable city of misconceptions,
   because though it appears to be clean when you
   wash it, as well as a source of bliss, permanent, and
   under your control, it is not. It is produced from the
   four elements (earth, water, fire, and wind), is subject to pain, and changes from moment to moment
   of its own accord.

3. People and things appear to exist under their own
   power, and ignorance accepts this false appearance,
   giving rise to the afflictive emotions of lust, hatred,
   and more bewilderment. These afflictive emotions
   in turn pollute actions of body, speech, and mind,

perpetuating the process of cyclic existence. Understand that you live in a city of misconceptions.

STANZA FIVE: WISHING FOR THE PACIFICATION OF
MISTAKEN APPEARANCES WHILE DYING (P. 103)

> *May we be relieved from mistaken appearances of*
>   *non-virtue*
> *When, deceived at the time of need by this body*
>   *sustained so dearly,*
> *The frightful enemies—the lords of death—manifest*
> *And we kill ourselves with the weapons of the three*
>   *poisons of lust, hatred, and bewilderment.*

1. Understand that this body, which you sustain at any cost, will someday desert you.
2. Avoid lusting after the situation you are leaving.
3. Avoid hating that you have to leave.
4. Keep away from lust, hatred, and ignorance as much as possible so that you can maintain virtuous practice while dying.
5. Realize that by taking a pill or an injection to have a so-called peaceful death you may be depriving yourself of a crucial opportunity for manifesting virtue.

STANZA SIX: WISHING FOR MINDFULNESS OF
INSTRUCTIONS WHILE DYING (P. 107)

> *May we remember instructions for practice*
> *When doctors forsake us and rites are of no avail,*
> *Friends have given up hope for our life,*
> *And we are left with nothing else to do.*

1. It is helpful to know that at some point all hope for continuing this life will end. At that point doctors, priests, friends, and relatives cannot keep you in this life; it will be up to you to do what helps.

2. While dying, you need to remember spiritual instructions that accord with your own level of practice and enact them.

3. Develop familiarity with your practice. Be determined to maintain this spiritual direction in all situations, no matter how difficult. Engage in many meritorious actions so that their accumulated force affects all aspects of your life and death. Realize that suffering arises from self-cherishing and learn to cherish others. Frequently wish to maintain your spiritual practice through future lives.

4. When another person dies, be careful not to upset him or her by causing more attachment or stirring

up anger and hatred. Do not bemoan their departure, grasp at them, or cry in their presence. Help them to depart meaningfully by reminding them of deeper practice.

5. If it is at all possible, ask others to do the same for you. Arrange to have someone near you who will speak softly into your ear from time to time, reminding you of a specific spiritual attitude that you want to manifest.

STANZA SEVEN: WISHING TO DIE WITHIN JOYFUL
CONFIDENCE (P. 112)

> *May we have the confidence of joy and delight*
> *When food and wealth accumulated with miserliness are*
> *   left behind*
> *And we separate forever from cherished and longed-for*
> *   friends,*
> *Going alone to a perilous situation.*

1. To avoid being depressed about dying, take refuge in your respective religion within compassion for all beings; reflect on the importance of extracting the essence of this present life, which is endowed with both the leisure and the necessities of spiritual

practice, and reflect again and again on impermanence.

2. With that groundwork for effectively remembering your practice while dying, even horrific events and appearances that might occur will only serve to urge you to be calm and to meditate with joy and confidence.

STANZA EIGHT: WISHING TO GENERATE A POWERFUL
MIND OF VIRTUE WHEN THE EXTERNAL SIGNS OF THE
DISSOLUTION OF THE ELEMENTS ARISE (P. 117)

> *May we generate a powerful mind of virtue*
> *When the elements—earth, water, fire, and wind—*
> *dissolve in stages*
> *And physical strength is lost, mouth and nose dry and*
> *pucker,*
> *Warmth withdraws, breaths are gasped, and rattling*
> *sounds emerge.*

1. So that you will not be surprised by the dying process when it starts, learn the stages of the dissolution of the four elements and their accompanying external and internal signs.

2. Take care near the time of death so that good pre-

dispositions are nourished and activated by virtuous attitudes.

3. Portents of death can appear within a year or two prior to dying. These alert you to the need to prepare, but it is better to be ready before then.

STANZA NINE: WISHING TO BE ABLE TO SUSTAIN REALIZATION OF THE PROFOUND REALITY WHEN THE INTERNAL SIGNS DAWN (P. 127)

May we realize the deathless mode of being
When various mistaken appearances frightful and
horrible
And in particular mirage, smoke, and fireflies appear
And the mounts of the eighty indicative conceptions cease.

1. Realize that the myriad appearances, some even frightening and horrible, which might occur while dying are due to karma. Do not be distracted by them.

2. Learn the first three of the eight appearances: mirage like that in a desert; puffs of smoke from a chimney or thin smoke throughout a room; fireflies, or sparks in the soot on the bottom of a wok.

STANZA TEN: WISHING TO GENERATE STRONG
MINDFULNESS OF FORMER VIRTUOUS ENDEAVOR WHEN
GROSS DUALISTIC APPEARANCE DISSOLVES (P. 129)

> *May we generate strong mindfulness and introspection*
> *When the wind constituent begins to dissolve into*
>   *consciousness*
> *And the external continuum of breath ceases, coarse*
>   *dualistic appearances dissolve,*
> *And an appearance like a burning butter lamp dawns.*

1. Although mind and matter have different substantial causes, they interact in many ways.
2. After the three internal signs of mirage, smoke, and fireflies, comes the fourth internal sign, which is like the flame of a butter lamp or of a candle, at first flickering and then steady.
3. Although at this point the outer breath through the nose ceases and there is no conscious reaction to external stimuli, the person has not died. It is helpful if the body is not disturbed until full death occurs.
4. Maintaining mindfulness and introspection that help you recognize which phase of the internal process is occurring can impel powerful realization and influence a positive rebirth.

STANZA ELEVEN: WISHING TO RECOGNIZE IN EXPERIENCE
THE NATURE OF YOUR OWN MIND WHEN THE FIRST
THREE EMPTIES MANIFEST (P. 135)

> May we know our own nature ourselves
> Through the yoga realizing cyclic existence and nirvana
>   as empty
> When appearance, increase, and near-attainment
>   dissolve—the earlier into the later—
> And experiences like pervasive moonlight, sunlight,
>   and darkness dawn.

1. Notice how various attitudes and conceptions have different strengths in terms of the movement of wind to their respective objects.

2. Learn that after the four internal signs of mirage, smoke, fireflies, and flame (of a butter lamp or of a candle, at first flickering and then steady), three more subtle minds of vivid white appearance, red-orange increase-of-appearance, and black near-attainment dawn.

3. Remember that you are seeking to use these more subtle minds to realize the truth of emptiness.

4. Emptiness does not mean nonexistence; rather, it is the lack of inherent existence of phenomena, both of beings and things.

5. Learn to analyze phenomena: Focus on whether they are any of their parts individually, or the collection of their parts, or something else entirely. This will show that phenomena do not exist in the concrete way they seem to.

6. All causes and effects, agents and actions, good and bad merely exist conventionally; they are dependent-arisings.

7. Their absence of independence, or emptiness of inherent existence, is their ultimate truth. This is what wisdom understands, undermining the ignorance behind lust and hatred and the suffering they cause.

8. Through this yoga know your own ultimate nature as well as that of all phenomena.

STANZA TWELVE: WISHING FOR THE MEETING OF THE MOTHER AND CHILD CLEAR LIGHTS DURING THE FOURTH EMPTY (P. 159)

> *May the mother and child clear lights meet*
> *When near-attainment dissolves into the all-empty*
> *And all conceptual multiplications cease and an*
>   *experience*
> *Like an autumn sky free from polluting conditions*
>   *dawns.*

1. The final phase in the process of dying occurs when the fundamental innate mind of clear light dawns. This mind has existed continuously since beginningless time and will continue to exist forever.

2. Eventually, at Buddhahood, you become capable of remaining in the innate mind of clear light without passing through the reverse process of the coarser levels of consciousness. At that point, there is no opportunity for the accumulation of karma.

3. Even for an ordinary non-practitioner, an absence of coarse appearances dawns at death, but a highly developed practitioner seeks to make use of this mind to realize the truth, the emptiness of inherent existence, through the force of familiarity gained from meditation on emptiness.

4. The ordinary mind of clear light that manifests in the final stage of death is called the mother clear light, and the clear light generated through the force of cultivating the spiritual path is called the child clear light.

5. When the mother clear light of death, which dawns due to karma, turns into a spiritual consciousness knowing emptiness—the child clear light—this

transformation is called the meeting of the mother and the child clear lights.

STANZA THIRTEEN: WISHING TO BE IN MEDITATIVE EQUIPOISE WITHIN THE EXALTED WISDOM OF BLISS AND EMPTINESS, JOINING INNATE BLISS AND EMPTINESS, DURING THE FOUR EMPTIES (P. 172)

May we be set in one-pointed profound meditation
In the exalted wisdom of joined innate bliss and emptiness
During the four empties upon the melting of the moon-
*   like white constituent*
By the fire of the lightning-like Powerful Female.

1. The highest level of practitioner can transform the mother clear light, which dawns at death due to karma, into a spiritual path consciousness.

2. On lower levels, those who daily practice the deity yoga of Highest Yoga Tantra imagine the appearance of the eight signs of death within a threefold mindfulness, identifying the sign that is appearing, the previous sign, and the one coming up. Practice the series of eight in conjunction with reflection on emptiness. Each has three parts except for the first and last, which have two:

- Mirage is appearing. Smoke is about to dawn.

- Smoke is appearing. Mirage just passed. Fireflies are about to dawn.

- Fireflies are appearing. Smoke just passed. A flame is about to dawn.

- A flame is appearing. Fireflies just passed. A vivid white appearance is about to dawn.

- A vivid white appearance is appearing. A flame just passed. A vivid red-orange increase is about to dawn.

- A vivid red-orange increase is appearing. A vivid white appearance just passed. A vivid blackness is about to dawn.

- A vivid blackness is appearing. A vivid red-orange increase just passed. The mind of clear light is about to dawn.

- The mind of clear light is appearing. A vivid blackness just passed.

3. In the particular practice of deity yoga in Highest Yoga Tantra, practitioners conjoin whatever level of understanding of emptiness they have with the gradual unfolding of the eight signs of death. Then they use the mind of clear light realizing empti-

ness—or a consciousness mimicking such a state of mind—as the basis out of which they appear in ideal, compassionate form as a deity.

4. Highly developed practitioners who have firm compassion and wisdom can make use of sexual intercourse as a technique to strongly focus the mind and manifest the fundamental innate mind of clear light. With this innermost mind they realize the emptiness of inherent existence in a dramatically powerful way.

STANZA FOURTEEN: WISHING TO ACHIEVE AN ILLUSORY BODY IN PLACE OF THE INTERMEDIATE STATE (P. 183)

May we complete in place of the intermediate state
The concentrated meditation of illusion so that upon
*   leaving the clear light*
We rise in a Body of Complete Enjoyment blazing with
*   the glory of a Buddha's marks and beauties*
Arisen from the mere wind and mind of the clear light
*   of death.*

1. Highly developed practitioners are able to utilize the common clear light of death and the wind on which it rides as the substantial causes of pure mind and body, respectively.

2. To be able to rise from within the mind of clear light in a pure body fashioned from wind, it is necessary to have previously practiced imagining yourself as having altruistically motivated mind and body. What is performed in imitation eventually leads to what is accomplished in fact.

3. Bringing about the final transformation requires not passing backward from the fundamental innate mind of clear light to a coarser level of mind. This yields a deathless state.

STANZA FIFTEEN: WISHING THAT ERRONEOUS
APPEARANCES DURING AN ORDINARY INTERMEDIATE
STATE APPEAR AS THE SPORT OF PURITY (P. 189)

> *If, due to karma, an intermediate state is established,*
> *May erroneous appearances be purified*
> *Through immediately analyzing and realizing the*
>   *absence of inherent existence*
> *Of the sufferings of birth, death, and intermediate*
>   *state.*

1. It is very important to recognize the signs that you are in the intermediate state.

2. View all pleasant and unpleasant appearances and

experiences as expressions of your own good and bad karma.

3. In place of what is presented to you, imagine that you have risen in an illusory body, imagining all appearances of beings as ideal expressions of compassion and wisdom and all appearances of environments as wondrous mansions.

4. Refrain from disliking the ugly or liking the beautiful.

5. Realize that the various appearances and sufferings of death, intermediate state, and rebirth are empty of inherent existence; they do not exist in their own right.

STANZA SIXTEEN: WISHING TO BE REBORN IN A PURE LAND THROUGH THE FORCE OF YOGA TRANSFORMING THE EXTERNAL, INTERNAL, AND SECRET (P. 194)

> May we be born in a pure land
> Through yoga transforming the external, internal,
>   and secret
> When various signs—four sounds of the reversal of
>   the elements,
> Three frightful appearances, and uncertainties—
>   appear.

1. Be prepared that in the intermediate state there may be many unusual appearances, both wonderful and horrific. Understand now that whatever appears can be transformed by practice.

2. Be calm. Imagine the environment as beautiful mansions laid out in a serene landscape. See beings as having an essence of compassion and wisdom. Consider your own awareness as a blissful mind realizing emptiness.

3. This will yield rebirth in a place where you can continue your practice toward deeper spiritual realization.

STANZA SEVENTEEN: WISHING TO BE REBORN IN A
MEANINGFUL WAY (P. 201)

> *May we be reborn with the supreme life support of a*
> *   Tantra practitioner using the sky*
> *Or the body of a monastic or lay practitioner possessing*
> *   the three practices*
> *And may we complete the realizations of the paths of the*
> *   two stages of generation and completion,*
> *Thereby attaining quickly a Buddha's Bodies—Truth,*
> *   Complete Enjoyment, and Emanation.*

1. Aim in your rebirth to be reborn with a body and in a situation capable of finishing the remaining spiritual paths.
2. The purpose of becoming fully enlightened is to fully serve others.

Selected Readings

H.H. the Dalai Lama, Tenzin Gyatso. *How to Practice: The Way to a Meaningful Life.* Translated and edited by Jeffrey Hopkins. New York: Pocket Books/Simon & Schuster, 2002.

———. *Kindness, Clarity, and Insight.* Translated and edited by Jeffrey Hopkins; coedited by Elizabeth Napper. Ithaca, N.Y.: Snow Lion Publications, 1984.

———. *The Meaning of Life.* Translated and edited by Jeffrey Hopkins. Boston: Wisdom Publications, 2000.

Hopkins, Jeffrey. *Buddhist Advice for Living and Liberation: Nagarjuna's Precious Garland.* Ithaca, N.Y.: Snow Lion Publications, 1998.

———. *Cultivating Compassion.* New York: Broadway Books, 2001.

Lekden, Kensur. *Meditations of a Tibetan Tantric Abbot.* Translated and edited by Jeffrey Hopkins. Ithaca, N.Y.: Snow Lion Publications, 2001.

Rinbochay, Lati, and Jeffrey Hopkins. *Death, Intermediate State and Rebirth in Tibetan Buddhism.* London: Rider, 1980; Ithaca, N.Y.: Snow Lion Publications, 1980.

Rinchen, Geshe Sonam, and Ruth Sonam. *Yogic Deeds of Bodhisattvas: Gyel-tsap on Aryadeva's Four Hundred.* Ithaca, N.Y.: Snow Lion Publications, 1994.

Tsongkhapa, *The Great Treatise on the Stages of the Path to Enlightenment,* vol. 1, trans. and ed. Joshua W. C. Cutler and Guy Newland. Ithaca, N.Y.: Snow Lion Publications, 2000; vol. 3, trans. and ed. Joshua W. C. Cutler and Guy Newland. Ithaca, N.Y.: Snow Lion Publications, 2002.

Wallace, Vesna A., and B. Alan Wallace. *A Guide to the Bodhisattva Way of Life.* Ithaca, N.Y.: Snow Lion Publications, 1997.